The Conquerors of Palestine Through Forty Centuries

MAJOR H.O. LOCK

INTRODUCTION BY VISCOUNT ALLENBY

NEW YORK

The Conquerors of Palestine Through Forty Centuries
First published in 1920.
Current edition published by Cosimo Classics in 2010.

Cover copyright © 2010 by Cosimo, Inc.

Cover design by www.popshopstudio.com
Cover image, "An Arab Caravan outside a Fortified Town, Egypt"
by Jean-Léon Gérôme.

ISBN: 978-1-61640-496-3

Cosimo aims to publish books that inspire, inform, and engage readers worldwide. We use innovative print-on-demand technology that enables books to be printed based on specific customer needs. This approach eliminates an artificial scarcity of publications and allows us to distribute books in the most efficient and environmentally sustainable manner. Cosimo also works with printers and paper manufacturers who practice and encourage sustainable forest management, using paper that has been certified by the FSC, SFI, and PEFC whenever possible.

Ordering Information:
Cosimo publications are available at online bookstores. They may also be purchased for educational, business, or promotional use:
Bulk orders: Special discounts are available on bulk orders for reading groups, organizations, businesses, and others.
Custom-label orders: We offer selected books with your customized cover or logo of choice.

For more information, contact us at:

Cosimo, Inc.
P.O. Box 416, Old Chelsea Station
New York, NY 10011

info@cosimobooks.com

or visit us at:
www.cosimobooks.com

The Author takes us along tracks well beaten by armies of old. We traverse the sands of Sinai, the plains of Philistia, of Sharon and Esdraelon. We scale the Mountains of Judea, of Samaria and Galilee. We descend to Jordan and the Dead Sea. We visit Jerusalem, Nazareth, Tyre, Sidon, Damascus, Aleppo. Every name is famous in history, sacred or profane. There is no locality that has not been the scene of mighty deeds and weighty issues.

—From The Introduction

CONTENTS

		PAGE
PREFACE	. . . .	vii
INTRODUCTION BY GENERAL SIR EDMUND ALLENBY	. .	ix

CHAP.
I	INTRODUCTORY	1
II	THE EGYPTIANS	7
III	THE JEWS (WARS OF THE EXODUS)	14
IV	THE JEWS (WARS OF THE JUDGES AND KINGS) . .	26
V	THE ASSYRIANS AND BABYLONIANS	35
VI	THE GREEKS	44
VII	THE ROMANS	53
VIII	THE ARABS	66
IX	THE CRUSADES	74
X	THE FRENCH	93
XI	THE BRITISH	100
XII	CONCLUSION	112
APPENDIX I		115
APPENDIX II		118

PREFACE

WHEN on active service in Palestine in 1917–18, I often felt, and heard others express, the want of a book, which, in small compass, would give an outline of the many previous invasions of that country. I have here set down matter collected from many sources, and woven together into a somewhat connected story, in the hope that it may be of interest to others who have fought or travelled, or are generally interested, in the Holy Land. I fully appreciate that, to do justice to a work like this, one needs to be antiquarian, theologian, and historian as well as soldier. I make no claim to be either of the former. But, having fought over the same ground, worked out the same problems, and experienced the same thrills, as the warriors of forty centuries, I have been emboldened to approach the subject at least from the point of view of the soldier.

I give a list of the authorities of which I have made use, in an appendix. In addition to references in the text and notes, I have ldrawn largely on the following, namely: Milman's *History of the Jews* for the earlier chapters; the *Works* of Josephus for Chapter VII; *The Caliphate*, by Sir Wm. Muir, for Chapter VIII; and *Jerusalem the city of Herod and Saladin*, by W. Besant and E. H. Palmer, for Chapter IX.

I appreciate that the arrangement of chapters which I have adopted is open to criticism on the ground of overlapping. Nevertheless, it is hoped that the arrangement adopted will conduce to simplicity, which is so essential in unravelling the tangled history of Palestine.

H. O. L.

ALEXANDRIA.

INTRODUCTION

BY FIELD-MARSHAL VISCOUNT ALLENBY, G.C.B., G.C.M.G.

MAJOR LOCK has achieved success in a difficult task. In one short book he has given to us a comprehensive and accurate historical summary of the campaigns which, from remote ages to our day, have had as their theatre the ancient battleground of Palestine.

Fresh interest has been added to Palestine by our recent campaign. Those who fought therein will read Major Lock's book with keen appreciation, and it will be equally welcomed by that great public which is appealed to by all relating to the Holy Land.

The Author takes us along tracks well beaten by armies of old. We traverse the sands of Sinai, the plains of Philistia, of Sharon and Esdraelon. We scale the Mountains of Judæa, of Samaria and Galilee. We descend to Jordan and the Dead Sea. We visit Jerusalem, Nazareth, Tyre, Sidon, Damascus, Aleppo. Every name is famous in history, sacred or profane. There is no locality that has not been the scene of mighty deeds and weighty issues.

To condense and to bring into historical form, within reach of the average reader, the great happenings of the ages, has entailed a labour that must have been colossal; but Major Lock will reap his reward in the gratitude of his readers.

ALLENBY.

CAIRO.

THE CONQUERORS OF PALESTINE
THROUGH FORTY CENTURIES
CHAPTER I
INTRODUCTORY

THE traveller, as he sets foot in Palestine, instinctively wonders what part each square mile has played in the military history of that country. He asks where the Crusaders fought and how came the Romans to the Holy Land. He thinks upon the battles of the Bible and conjures up the familiar scenes in their appropriate setting. Still more does he wish to fit each Palestinian war into its place in history, and to understand the influence which each invasion exercised upon subsequent invasions and upon the country and people as a whole. The object of this book is to present, in one small volume, an outline of the principal conquests of that much-conquered country; and, side by side, to depict the battles of the ancients, the battles of the middle ages, and the battles of to-day.

When campaigning in Palestine, one is struck by the recurrence of many of the identical problems which presented themselves to the ancients. The wars of the Bible acquire added interest when read in the light of to-day.

Let us consider, as examples, the problems of water and transport.

Palestine is separated from Egypt by a stretch of barren desert over a hundred miles across. In a few places water can be found in wells; in some places the winter rainfall is stored in cisterns; but for the greater part of its extent this desert is waterless. When the Turks invaded Egypt in 1915, and when the British retaliated by invading Palestine, one of the foremost difficulties that had to be overcome was the supply of water. Much ingenuity was exercised in overcoming this difficulty; and the only satisfactory way by which a constant ample supply could be maintained for the British Army was by laying a pipe-line across the desert and pumping through it water from the Nile. Every army that has invaded Palestine from Egypt, or vice versa, must have crossed that desert, and must have solved for itself this problem of water. Esarhaddon, for example, going down to invade Egypt centuries before Christ, carried water upon the backs of camels, a method used by the British in 1917 for local distribution from the pipe-head and water dumps to the fighting units. This water supply difficulty was one of the chief stumbling-blocks of the Israelites when they came up out of Egypt, for they murmured against Moses and said, "Wherefore is this that thou hast brought us up out of Egypt to kill us and our children and our cattle with thirst?"[1] Conditions have so far altered that we now eat bully beef and ration biscuits instead of quails and manna, but the problem of water is ever present.

The question of transport is one of never-failing importance. Consider the advantages and disadvantages, in such a country as this, of pack as against wheeled transport. Upon good roads or across hard country, relatively more can be carried in wheeled carts than on the backs of pack animals. But who is there that has marched with a mixed column and has not wished his wheeled vehicles at perdition, when deep mud or soft sand has been encountered? It is probable that, when Israel came out of Egypt, their baggage was carried upon pack

[1] Exodus xvii. 3.

INTRODUCTORY

animals according to the custom of Eastern caravans, and that they were not encumbered with transport wagons or weapons of war on wheels. The Egyptians, on the other hand, "took six hundred chosen chariots, and all the chariots of Egypt," and brought these forward in pursuit. So long as the route lay across firm ground the well-horsed Egyptian chariots had no difficulty in overtaking the slow-going Israelites. But mark the difference when the Red Sea mud or sand had to be passed. The Israelites got across without difficulty. The heavy war-chariots of the Egyptians sunk or stuck in the mud, and the wheels were wrenched off, so "that they drave them heavily." Panic overcame the Egyptians, "the waters returned, and covered the chariots and the horsemen and all the host of Pharaoh."

How well do I recollect marching with a column across firm desert, when, without warning, we found ourselves ploughing through soft sand. Our artillery and most of our baggage was on pack animals, but our ambulances were of a heavy wheeled type drawn by bullocks. Although the soft sand was but a belt, little more than half a mile wide, it took hours to drag these ambulances across, the whole column being thereby delayed. Had the enemy chosen this moment to attack, he would have caught us at a manifest disadvantage, comparable to that of the chariot-encumbered Egyptians when overwhelmed by the waters of the Red Sea.

Before embarking upon our consideration of the several campaigns of Palestine, it is necessary that we should devote a passing reference to the geography of this Battlefield of Nations.

Palestine may be defined as that tract of country which reaches from the southern bases of the Lebanon and Anti-Lebanon ranges to the southern shores of the Dead Sea and the border of the Desert. Syria, in its wider sense, comprises the eastern boundary of the Mediterranean from the confines of Asia Minor in the north to the border of Egypt and the peninsula of Sinai in the south, and thus includes Palestine. In its more restricted sense, Syria refers only to the portion north of Palestine, and this is the sense in which we find it generally used in the Bible. In the pages of this book the sense in which the name 'Syria' is used, will, it is hoped, sufficiently appear from the context.

Approximately the natural, but ill-defined, boundaries of Palestine are the hill countries of Lebanon on the north, the Mediterranean Sea on the west, and the deserts of Arabia and Sinai on the east and south. Across the north, extending from the sea at Acre and Haifa on the north-west to the Jordan Valley at Beisan on the south-east, runs the Plain of Esdraelon, the Armageddon of the World. On its south-western side this plain of Esdraelon is enclosed by the Carmel range and the northern slope of the mountains of Samaria, forming an almost continuous elevated chain from Cape Carmel on the sea to Mount Gilboa overlooking Beisan and the Jordan. Eastward of the Jordan, and a few miles further north, is the gorge of the Yarmuk River. Thus we get an irregular cross formed by the Jordan Valley running north and south, with, as its arms, the gorge of the Yarmuk and the Plain of Esdraelon.

South of this cross, the country is divided longitudinally into alternate zones of elevation and depression. Bordering on the sea is the fertile maritime plain, known towards the north as the Plain of Sharon, and towards the south as the Plain of Philistia. This plain, the home of the Jaffa orange, is the great highway between Asia and Africa. To the east of the maritime plain come the range of foothills known as the Shephelah, through which one rises into the continuous range of hills known towards the north as the Mountains of Ephraim or Samaria, and to the south as the Mountains of Judæa. These rise to a height of from two to three thousand feet above sea level, and, perched upon them, are such familiar cities as Samaria (in ruins), Nablus (Shechem), Jerusalem, Bethlehem, and Hebron. From this mountain

INTRODUCTORY

range the country falls precipitously for some four thousand feet to the Valley of the Jordan and the Dead Sea. This depression, unique upon the face of the globe, lies more than a thousand feet below normal sea-level. Eastward of the Jordan Valley the country rises again as abruptly to the mountains of Moab and Ammon. But it falls no more. At first fertile, where it is reached by the rains of the Mediterranean, it passes gradually into pastoral regions, and then, as one goes further East, into steppe and highland pastures, until at length it merges in the limitless desert of Arabia.

The plains are easily passable for wheeled traffic, but through the hills the good roads are limited to two, the one running north and south, the other east and west, which cross at Jerusalem. The railways, largely the product of the 1914–1918 War, follow the line of the time-honoured route from Damascus up the Plain of Esdraelon and down the coastal plain, through Gaza, and so on to Egypt. Branch lines climb up to Jerusalem and to Nablus. East of the Jordan, the Hejaz railway follows the caravan route from Damascus down to Medina and Mecca.

Rivers, except in the Jordan Valley, are almost non-existent. There is a copious rainfall throughout the winter, averaging from twenty to thirty inches, but the summer months are absolutely rainless. Except between seasons, campaigning in this country is liable to be seriously hampered, in the winter by storms at sea and quagmires on land, and in the summer by the difficulties of procuring water at all. It will be understood that the watercourses, dry in summer, form in winter little more than surface-water drains. There are two or three small perennial streams flowing into the Mediterranean, which derive their supply from springs, the best known of which is the river Kishon. Although generally riverless, the country is by no means waterless. Much water is stored up by the absorbent soil from the copious winter rains, a few good springs are to be found in the hills, while on the coastal plain wells are plentiful.

A country with such varying altitudes enjoys, as might be expected, a diversity of climates. On the whole, the climate is equable and not unsuited to military life in the open, except during the winter rains. The climate in the Jordan Valley, though pleasant enough in winter, is in the summer almost unbearable. Malignant malaria is very prevalent in the Jordan Valley, and on the coastal plain from September onwards. Napoleon, who was not in Palestine in September, suffered nothing from malaria. Richard, in the Crusades, suffered severely from malaria, as did the Turks, and to some extent the British, in 1918. Napoleon, on the other hand, suffered from plague and ophthalmia, diseases which are still prevalent in Palestine.

Forming a narrow passage between the Mediterranean and the Desert, Palestine was the only natural highway between the Euphrates and the Nile, between Asia and Africa. Along this highway passed the caravans of peace and the cohorts of war. There is probably no country in the world that has so often fallen a victim to foreign invasion.

CHAPTER II

THE EGYPTIANS

THE romantic history of Joseph in Egypt forms, for most of us, our first introduction to the ancient civilization of the Nile. We start with the vivid contrast of the two Pharaohs, the one who welcomed Joseph advancing him to honour, and the other who "knew not Joseph" but oppressed Israel. These two Pharaohs represent entirely distinct periods and regimes in the history of Egypt; their reigns were separated by a period of about five centuries.

"Egypt for the Egyptians"[1] was a state of affairs that seems to have existed for two or three thousand years, from before the days of the Pyramid builders down to the fourteenth dynasty. Then Egypt fell a prey to invaders from Asia who overran the country, devastating it with fire and sword, destroying most of the previous monuments and works of art and probably rifling the Pyramids. These Asiatic invaders established a dynasty, the fifteenth, which is known as that of the Hyksos or Shepherd kings. How long this alien dynasty lasted is uncertain; estimates put its duration at several centuries. These foreign rulers gradually assimilated Egyptian manners and customs, and, by the end of the dynasty, they had become thoroughly Egyptianized. It was probably during the reign of the last of these Shepherd kings, that Joseph came down into Egypt and rose into power. It will readily be understood how acceptable the immigration of Joseph and his relations from Syria would be to one of these Shepherd kings, himself of Asiatic extraction. The grip

---

[1] This cry was being raised by the crowd outside my windows in Alexandria as these pages were being written.

of these alien Shepherd or Hyksos kings, which had never been much more than nominal over Upper Egypt, gradually relaxed also upon Lower Egypt and the Delta. Somewhere about two thousand years before Christ, the king of Upper Egypt, joining to his standard the Ethiopians of the Soudan and the Egyptian peoples of Lower Egypt, succeeded in throwing off the foreign yoke, driving out the ruling Asiatics and forcing them to withdraw to the land of their origin in Asia.

Thothmes I, who was the first Egyptian king to embark upon Asiatic conquest, was a grandson of the king of Upper Egypt who had driven out the Hyksos. He must have inherited much of his grandfather's spirit of military adventure. He first embarked upon an expedition towards the Upper Nile. Having achieved success in that direction, he turned his eyes towards Asia. Here was an inviting field for the exercise of his military ambition, and an opportunity to pay off an old score against the Hyksos. Accordingly he emerged from the fertile valley of the Nile, and led his forces across the eastern desert to Palestine. He must have encountered the Philistines and the Canaanities, and other small Syrian tribes of no great military importance. He seems to have carried his victories as far as the Euphrates, whence he returned to Egypt, bringing with him a goodly booty and a vast number of Asiatic prisoners. It is difficult to fix the dates of these early invasions, but we shall be approximately correct if we call this date about two thousand years before Christ. Thothmes I may have been a remarkable man; he certainly begat remarkable offspring, in his daughter Hatasu and his son Thothmes III, both, in turn, sovereigns of Egypt. Hatasu, having first married and then probably assassinated, her brother Thothmes II, reigned nominally as regent for her younger brother, Thothmes III, but in effect with the power and energy of a tyrant. She was a great builder, and travellers to-day are charmed to gaze upon the temples which she erected at Thebes. She organized expeditions, both by land and sea, the objects of which seem to have been commercial rather than military. The pictorial description of her great expedition to the land of Punt, as depicted upon the walls of her temple at Luxor, is delightful.

Thothmes III was a man of great ambition and no less ability, and he must have chafed at the position which he occupied while his overbearing sister exercised despotic power. Brotherly and sisterly affection scarcely existed. Hatasu had probably murdered her elder brother Thothmes II. On her own death or disappearance, her younger brother Thothmes III caused her name to be erased from all her monuments, in the hope that her remembrance might perish from the pages of history.

[1] " No sooner had Thothmes III burst the leading strings in which his sister had held him for above twenty years, than he showed the mettle of which he was made by at once placing himself at the head of his troops, and marching into Asia. Persuaded that the great god Ammon had promised him a long career of victory, he lost no time in setting to work to accomplish his glorious destiny. Starting from an Egyptian post on the eastern frontier in the month of February, he took his march along the ordinary coast route, and in a short time reached Gaza, the strong Philistine city, which was already a fortress of repute, and regarded as the key of Syria. The day of his arrival was the anniversary of his coronation, and according to his reckoning the first day of his twenty-third year. Gaza made no resistance ; its chief was friendly to the Egyptians and gladly opened his gates to the invading army. Having rested at Gaza no more than a single night, Thothmes resumed his march, and, continuing to skirt the coast, arrived on the eleventh day at a fortified town called Jaham, probably Jamnia. Here he was met by his scouts, who brought the intelligence that the enemy was collected at Megiddo, on

[1] *Ancient Egypt*, by George Rawlinson.

the edge of the great plain of Esdraelon, the ordinary battlefield of the Palestinian nations. They consisted of "all the people dwelling between the [1] river of Egypt on the one hand and the land of Naharain (Mesopotamia) on the other." At their head was the king of Kadesh, a great city on the Upper Orontes, which afterwards became one of the chief seats of the Hittite power, but was at this time in the possession of the Rutennu (Syrians). They were strongly posted at the mouth of a narrow pass, behind the ridge of hills which connects Carmel with the Samaritan upland, and Thothmes was advised by his captains to avoid a direct attack and march against them by a circuitous route, which was undefended. But the intrepid warrior scorned this prudent counsel. "His generals," he said, "might take the roundabout road, if they liked; *he* would follow the straight one!" The event justified his determination. Megiddo was reached in a week without loss or difficulty, and a great battle was fought on the fertile plain to the north-west of the fortress, in which the Egyptian king was completely victorious, and his enemies were scattered like chaff before him. The Syrians must have fled precipitately at the first attack; for they lost in killed no more than 83 and in prisoners no more than 240, or according to another account 340, while the chariots taken were 924, and the captured horses 2,132. Megiddo was near at hand, and the bulk of the fugitives would reach easily the shelter of its walls. Others may have dispersed themselves among the mountains. The Syrian camp was, however, taken, together with vast treasures in silver and gold, lapis lazuli, turquoise, and alabaster; and the son of the king of Kadesh fell into Thothmes' hands. Megiddo itself, soon afterwards, with other towns surrendered. An immense booty in corn and cattle was also carried off. Thothmes returned to Egypt in triumph.

[1] The "River of Egypt" frequently referred to in Scripture, is nôt, as might be supposed, the river Nile, but the Wady el Arish, which forms the natural north-eastern frontier of Egypt.

Thothmes' expeditions into Asia appear to have been repeated almost yearly. In the following year we find him traversing the whole of Syria and ravaging the country about Aleppo, whence he proceeded to Carchemish, the great Hittite town on the Upper Euphrates, where he crossed into Mesopotamia. Sometimes he marched across the desert. Sometimes he brought his men up by sea, making piratical descents upon the coast. The primary object of these expeditions seems to have been the capture of slaves and booty. He by no means confined himself to filibustering raids near home however, but pushed on to the Euphrates and Tigris where he insulted and challenged the great powers of Mesopotamia.

Although he may not have conquered Assyria and Babylon, yet he for a time administered a severe check to Assyrian aggression, and even succeeded in extracting a tribute or compulsory annual gift from the monarch of Assyria. He seems to have annexed part of the Mesopotamian region and occupied it with a garrison, for some of his expeditions were directed against his rebellious subjects in that area. A military road was kept open between Egypt and Mesopotamia, and the Rutennu or Syrians, through whose countries it ran, had to supply the stations along the road with provisions, and had also to give hostages to Egypt for their own good behaviour. After Thothmes' death his son Amenhotep carried on the good work, keeping the subject races in Asia in order with sundry exhibitions of barbarity.

One of the chief powers of Western Asia about this time was that of the Hittites. During the campaigns of Thothmes, the Hittites probably retired into their mountain fastnesses. But when the Egyptian activities became less pronounced, they appear to have emerged and to have reigned as lords paramount over the entire region between the Middle Euphrates and the Mediterranean, the Taurus Range and the borders of Egypt. The Egyptians had been occupied with domestic troubles. When they were able once more to think imperially, they awoke to the aggression of the Hittites, and plunged again into those dominions. The Hittite king accepted the challenge. The Egyptians under Seti I moved into Asia against the Hittites, taking them by surprise. He overran the buffer states of Palestine, and met the main army of the Hittites beyond Kadesh on the Orontes. In the battle that followed the Egyptians were successful, but by the subsequent treaty Northern Syria remained under the dominion of the Hittites.

Although the Egyptians were restored to most of their Asiatic possessions yet Seti realized the danger of the rising tide of Hittite aggression. Accordingly we find him constructing a defensive wall from Pelusium, on the Mediterranean a little to the east of where now stands Port Said, to Pithom or Hereopolis, where began the long line of lagoons connected with the upper end of the Red Sea.

Seti was succeeded by his son Rameses II, who was the greatest builder, and at the same time the greatest plagiarist, of all the kings of Egypt. His name is to be found on most of the ancient Egyptian monuments, not only on those which he himself built, but on many of earlier date for which he wished to appropriate the credit. He devoted himself to the construction of great public works; incidentally he is believed to have been the Pharaoh who oppressed Israel. We read of the Israelites that "they built for Pharaoh treasure cities, Pithom and Rameses." The "treasure cities" were probably store cities or depots, possibly part of the defensive works which had been begun by his father Seti.

Rameses had in his veins some of the fighting blood of his ancestors. The Hittite king having commenced a series of intrigues with the nations bordering on Upper Syria and formed a confederacy for the purpose of resisting the further progress of the Egyptians, Rameses marched into Syria. A pitched battle was fought, again near Kadesh on the Orontes. Rameses appears to have been victorious. But either his victory cost him too dear, or, for other reasons of prudence, he accepted the surrender of the Hittites and agreed to withdraw. Later an alliance was entered into with the Hittites, cemented by the marriage of Rameses with a daughter of the Hittite king. From this time forth the influence of the Egyptians in Asia grew vague and shadowy. At long intervals more enterprising monarchs asserted it, and a brief success generally crowned their efforts. Speaking broadly, it may be said that her Asiatic dominion was lost, and that Egypt became once more a power confined within her ancient limits in Africa.

We are now in a position to understand how and why it came about that " there arose up a new king over Egypt that knew not Joseph." During the five centuries or so that had elapsed since their immigration, the Israelites must have grown into a populous, though not necessarily very warlike, tribe. With the racial exclusiveness common to the Jew even to this day, they had doubtless retained their foreign Asiatic characteristics and purity of blood. They must have occupied a position of long-suffering persecution in a strange land, similar to their descendants the Jews of Mediæval Europe.

To Rameses, then, these Israelities appeared as alien immigrants, imported into his country during a regime, the very recollection of which was distasteful to loyal Egyptians. He must have regarded them as thoroughly Asiatic both in extraction and sympathies. We have seen that the enemy mostly to be feared in these days were the Asiatic Hittites, possibly the representatives of the very Hyksos who had shown such favour to Israel. Can it be wondered at then, that Rameses should have exclaimed, " Behold, the people of the children of Israel are more and mightier than we. Come on, let us deal wisely with them ; lest they multiply, and it come to pass, that, when there falleth out any war, they join also unto our enemies, and fight against us." [1]

[1] Exodus i. 9, 10.

CHAPTER III

THE JEWS

(WARS OF THE EXODUS)

RAMESES was succeeded by his son Menephthah, a feeble monarch, born under an unlucky star. In the fifth year of his reign he had to meet a formidable attack from a combination of nations, the like of which we do not again meet with in Egyptian history. The invasion came this time, not from Asia, but from the western desert, Libya. The motive of the invaders, like that of the Hyksos, appears to have been to effect a settlement in the tempting valley of the Nile. The blow fell upon the western side of the Delta, and was at first completely successful. The Libyans and their allies ravaged the open country; Egypt was desolated. Eventually the king, who had been taking refuge at Memphis, sent an army against the Libyan invaders, and succeeded in driving them out and restoring some sort of tranquillity to Egypt.

It must have been shortly after this recovery that Moses demanded for the Israelites permission to migrate from Egypt, the land of their bondage. Egypt's extremity was Israel's opportunity. Menephthah alternately promised and retracted, until at last his consent was only wrung from him by his terror of the Plagues. He proved himself that worst of all rulers, a weak and vacillating tyrant. What pictures are not conjured up in the imagination as one gazes upon those lips that exclaimed, "I know not the Lord, neither will I let Israel go," and upon the face of him who cried out to Moses saying, "Get thee from me, take heed to thyself, see my face no more: for in that day thou seest my face thou shalt die."[1]

The Israelites, who were settled in the land of Goschen, in the Delta, moved off and journeyed from Rameses to Succoth. Menephthah, changing his mind again, started off in pursuit and overtook the Israelite host on the western shores of the Red Sea. The exact spot cannot be fixed, but it was probably some part of the region that is now dry land, between Suez and the southern extremity of the Bitter Lakes, where, in high tides, the sea and the lakes then communicated. On this fateful evening, an unusual ebb of the tide, co-operating with a strong east wind, which held back the water of the Bitter Lakes, left the bed of the sea bare. The Israelites were thus able to cross during the night from one side of the sea to the other. As morning dawned the Egyptian chariots followed in hot pursuit. The force entered on the slippery and dangerous ground, and advanced half-way; but its progress was slow; the chariot wheels sank into the soft ooze, the horses slipped and floundered; all was disorder and confusion. A sudden change of the wind probably occurred, driving down the waters of the Bitter Lakes to meet the high flood tide from the Gulf of Suez. The channel, which had lately been dry land, became once more sea, and the entire force of the Egyptians that had entered it in pursuit of the Israelites perished.[2]

Sir William Willcocks, in his fascinating work,[3] contends that the crossing must have taken place considerably further to the north, that the words translated "Red Sea" should rather be "reedy water," and that the event occurred in the marshes about the lower waters of the Pelusiac branch of the Nile. In his opinion the Israelites dammed the river and

---

[1] The mummied body of Menephthah is now one of the highly prized treasures of the Museum at Cairo.
[2] *Ancient Egypt*, by George Rawlinson.
[3] *From the Garden of Eden to the Crossing of the Jordan*.

then, when the Egyptians were well advanced into the boggy ground, cut the dam and so ensured their destruction. Whether the passage occurred to the south-east of Ismailia at the Bitter Lakes, or to the north-west near Lake Menzala, in either case the principle is the same. It is not necessary to believe that the crossing occurred at the deep sea waters of the Gulf of Suez, or that the waters stood up on either side as a wall in any more literal sense of the word than that in which Shakespeare speaks of Britain as " set in the silver sea which serves it in the office of a wall."

The Israelites moved out into the Desert, and their difficulties soon commenced. The first trouble was with the water, which at Maráh was found to be bitter. But Moses, whose genius at overcoming water difficulties was not the least of his qualifications for the leadership of a host moving across the desert, threw in a tree and the water was made sweet. It is suggested that he threw in the berry of a shrub growing in the neighbourhood, and thus sweetened the water. Sir William Willcocks, on the other hand, suggests that Moses rendered the water potable by making a dam of trees, thereby either cutting off an influx of brackish water, or diverting a water-course of fresh water into a depression which was thus made to serve as a reservoir.

Their next difficulty was that of supplies. Admittedly they had come up to live on the country, a course impossible for a modern army, and at no time easy upon this wild desert. Manna, or sweet tamarisk, now very rare, was found by them in abundance. Quails were sent them for food. Quails still fly across the Mediterranean and drop down in myriads exhausted on the northern shores of Africa, where their capture forms a considerable industry. This, according to Sir William Willcocks, proves that the Israelites encamped by the Mediterranean. The itinerary which he suggests is by the coast route as far as El Arish, and thence down the Wadi El Arish to Kadesh Barnea, which is identified with Ain Kadis about

THE JEWS (WARS OF THE EXODUS)

50 miles south of Beersheba. He places the whole of the wandering of the Israelites in the desert to the north of the Gulf of Akaba, where sufficient water-bearing oases are to be found. He considers it highly improbable that they moved as far south as the waterless Mt. Sinai near the southern extremity of the Peninsula.

The Israelites did not follow the coast route, the way of the Philistines, which was, and still is, the normal caravan route between Egypt and Syria. They probably followed it as far as El Arish before turning towards the south. They did not go straight up into Philistia because Moses feared that when the people saw the necessity of fighting they would lose heart and return to Egypt. Almost every army that has invaded Palestine has found it necessary to fight a battle at Gaza; perhaps it was such a battle that the Israelites turned southward to avoid.

After two years in the desert we find them again at Kadesh Barnea. We can understand that Moses may well have been more inclined now to attempt the invasion of Palestine. When the host first came up, they had but recently been liberated from bondage. It is doubtful whether they would then have formed any better fighting material than the personnel of the Egyptian Labour Corps to-day. But after two years' sojourn in the desert they must have become considerably hardened; while the likelihood of their returning to Egypt was correspondingly decreased.

Accordingly Moses now contemplated an advance into Palestine. He wisely took steps to make his "intelligence" as reliable as possible before embarking on the campaign. He therefore sent out a reconnoitring patrol. It is interesting to note how precise were the instructions given as to the points on which information was required. This patrol went out by the Desert of Sin and up as far as Lebanon returning through Hebron, their reconnaissance having taken them forty days. They reported that the land was rich and flowing with milk and honey, but that it was inhabited by warlike tribes who would prove more than a match for the people of Israel. Accordingly Moses decided that the immediate invasion was not practicable.

The Israelites remained in the Desert for a period of "forty years"[1] before they embarked in earnest upon their campaign of conquest. In the meantime all the fighting men that came out of Egypt had died off or grown too old to take a very active part in the operations. A fresh generation had grown up. The fighting men of this period were desert born and bred, wilder and hardier than the men of an ex-coolie stamp who had come out of Egypt. It has been suggested that, during their forty years wanderings in the wilderness, the Israelites had probably hired themselves out as free-lances ready to fight for anyone making them a good offer, and that in this way they had all learnt the art of war which now served them so well.[2]

The starting point for the invasion of Palestine was again Kadesh Barnea. As before, the Israelites did not seek to enter Palestine by the coastal route common to most invading armies. On the contrary they decided to march round the Dead Sea and approach the country from the East. It may be asked why they did not simply march due north from Kadesh Barnea into the hill-country, the goal of their ambitions, straight up through Beersheba and Hebron. The answer is that this country was mountainous, fortified and inhabited by a war-like people. Moreover the country is to this day one in which the difficulty of water supply makes campaigning impossible. According to Dr. George Adam Smith,[3] the hill country of Judæa has almost never been

---

[1] The period "forty years," frequently met with in the Bible, means, not so much a definite period of that duration, but rather a considerable period of time, the exact duration of which is unknown.

[2] Sir William Willcocks, *From the Garden of Eden to the Crossing of the Jordan.*

[3] *The Historical Geography of the Holy Land.*

THE JEWS (WARS OF THE EXODUS) 19

invaded from the South. Although in the operations for the capture of Jerusalem by the British in 1917 a division advanced on Jerusalem by this route, the enemy had been previously drawn off elsewhere, and its advance was unopposed.

In order to gain the highlands on the eastern side of the Dead Sea it was necessary for the Israelites to pass round or through the land of Edom, the high ridge on the south or south-east of the Dead Sea, bordering on the Desert of Arabia. Terms were offered to the Edomites resembling those offered by Germany to Belgium and Luxemburg in 1914. If the Edomites would permit the free passage of the Israelite host through their country, the host would pass through on terms of strict neutrality. The Edomites refused and offered armed opposition. The Israelites therefore made a circuitous march southwards as far as the head of the Gulf of Akabah, the eastern arm of the Red Sea. From here they turned north-east, striking the caravan route from Medina to Damascus somewhere near Maan. They were then upon the line now followed by the Hejaz railway. Moving approximately up the Hejaz railway route, they circumvented Edom, thus taking the Edomites on their open flank, from whom they encountered no further resistance. The army passed through Moab, the mountainous country immediately to the East of the Dead Sea, meeting at this time with little or no opposition, and met and defeated Sihon and the Amorites. Then they defeated Og the king of Basan whose country lay further to the north; and thus they possessed themselves of the whole country to the east of the river Jordan, up to or beyond the River Jabbok, the Wadi Zerka of the present day. Returning south again they met the Moabites, who, now genuinely alarmed at the invasion, had mustered their forces to offer determined opposition. Now it was, and at a spot not far from the north-east corner of the Dead Sea, that Balaam failed in his task of cursing the host, and poured forth his blessing instead, to the disgust of his patron, the Moabitish king, Balak. Another great battle was fought in which the Israelites completely defeated the Moabites and their desert allies the Midianites. Although these peoples were but little peoples, and their territories no larger than an average English county, yet, through the pages of scripture and the pæans of the Psalmists, the fame of these battles is more widely known than that of Creasy's Decisive Battles of the World.

It was here in full view of the mountains of Judæa that the aged Moses breathed his last, and the warrior Joshua, who had hitherto been commander-in-chief, now succeeded to the supreme command of the host. Preparations were made for the passage of the river Jordan, and invasion of Judæa. Before attempting the passage, Joshua prudently took measures to obtain all the information of military value that he could procure as to the country across the river and the opposition likely to be encountered. Two spies were sent across who penetrated into the city of Jericho. Here they obtained much useful information at the house of Rahab, the harlot. These spies brought back word that the people of Jericho were in a state of panic at the approach of the Israelites, terrified by the military reputation which the latter had acquired through their victories over the tribes upon the eastern side of the river. No serious military opposition therefore seemed likely to be encountered.

The crossing of the river Jordan, with a military force and in flood time, is an operation of the greatest difficulty. On this occasion it appears to have been much simplified by the cutting off of the upper waters. According to Sir Wm. Willcocks' theory, an earthquake occurred which caused a landslide further up the valley, a mass of earth being deposited in the river bed sufficient temporarily to dam up the waters; which earthquake may incidentally have also shaken the city walls of Jericho to their foundations contributing to their subsequent collapse. The fact remains that the host crossed the river without serious difficulty and encamped at Gilgal upon the western side in readiness for their offensive against Jericho.

At this time Canaan was split up into a number of small tribes or settlements, each small hill town being under a separate ruler or "king." At first no attempt at combination was made to resist the invasion. Jericho had alone to bear the brunt of the shock. Siege was laid to the city, and the morale of the wretched inhabitants was so low that the victory was won by the Israelites almost before the battle commenced. After a spectacular demonstration, the city was carried by assault, the assaulting troops pouring through the breach in the wall. Then the city was burnt and the inhabitants massacred to a man, with the exception of the harlot traitress Rahab, whose life, with that of her relations, was spared as the reward for her treachery.

The proceedings after the fall of Jericho are not without their modern parallels. There can be no question as to the wisdom of Joshua in requiring such of the loot as was to be preserved to be brought into a common fund. Thus the silver and gold and the vessels of brass and iron were brought "into the treasury of the house of the Lord." Whether the cattle were slain as a measure of expediency, or as part of a policy of intimidation, is not clear. It is reasonable to suppose, however, that the carcases were eaten and not merely wasted. The punishment of Achan, though drastic, has its equivalent in the provisions of our own Army Act.

From Jericho the Israelites moved up into the mountains of Judæa. They did not follow the route to Jerusalem. In fact Jerusalem appears not to have possessed at that time sufficient importance to form the goal of their invasion. They took a more northerly route through Michmash, aiming at the commanding position about El Bireh, which formed the objective of the British army in 1917. By means of a stratagem they captured the city of Ai. Here again the conquerors butchered the unfortunate inhabitants, men and women, the poor king of Ai being hanged on a tree.

And now at last the scattered chiefs of the Canaanite towns, the "kings" of Jerusalem, Hebron, Jarmath, Lachish and Eglon, formed a coalition against Israel. The citizens (or should we rather say the townsmen or villagers) of Gibeon, the modern El Jib, having forestalled the Israelites, and saved themselves by entering into a somewhat degrading treaty with Israel, this action was used as a pretext by the five "kings." The coalition came up and fought against Gibeon. The Gibeonites at once sent for the Israelites whose headquarters were still at Gilgal. Up came the Israelites into the hills, executing a night march and taking the enemy by surprise, and won an overwhelming victory. The stricken Canaanites fled down the Valley of Ajalon, that valley leading down from El Jib to the plain near Ramleh and Ludd. The completeness of their discomfiture was ensured by the pursuit which the Israelites carried out with the assistance of an abnormally prolonged daylight and a violent hailstorm. By this victory the first great organized Canaanitish opposition which the Israelites had to encounter was completely overthrown.

The Israelites now set out upon a tour of conquest, or, rather, as it seems to us, of wanton destruction, capturing and destroying the cities of Southern Judæa and putting their inhabitants to the sword.

Yet another pitched battle was fought against the northern chieftains, who were defeated at the Waters of Merom. The conquered territory was then portioned out among the tribes and the war ceased. But though the great war ceased, the country could not be said to be wholly subdued, nor the conquered territory consolidated. It was scarcely a tranquil country, therefore, which Joshua left behind him when he died at the good old age of over a century.

The humanely-minded Christian, reading the Biblical account

of the invasion of the Promised Land by the Israelites, is pained and puzzled to understand the wholesale massacres of the inhabitants, in which the conquerors indulged in compliance with the wishes of God. The Christian's conception of God is that which he receives from the teaching of Christ. He looks upon Him as the loving Father, who clothes the lilies of the field, watches over the sparrows, comforts the distressed, and desires not the death of a sinner but rather that he may turn from his wickedness and live.

The times of which we write were times of conquest and invasion. The mightiest invaders of those days, who have passed on their records to us, were the Egyptians and the Assyrians. The principal motives which prompted those conquerors were the capture of loot and of slaves, and their wars were accompanied with gross acts of cruelty. We have only to look at the sculptures on the Egyptian temples that have come down to us, and which were doubtless seen by the Israelites before they left Egypt, to see such incidents ostentatiously depicted as the slaughter of captives taken in war, or the counting of the severed hands of victims to ascertain the numbers of the captured or slain. If this was the school of military morals in which the Israelites and their ancestors had been brought up, they probably marched out of Egypt with brutal ideas as to the appropriate method of dealing with any enemies whom they might overcome. Such ideas would doubtless become hardened rather than mollified by the forty years privations in the Desert.

Moreover the Israelites had no use for a large number of slaves. Their expedition was not a slave raid but a colonizing migration. The Gibeonites, the hewers of wood and drawers of water, were sufficient for their servile purposes. It suited the Israelites' programme much better that the remainder of the population should not be kept alive, but rather should be exterminated that their lands might be occupied by the immigrants. The wild Judæan hills are not capable of supporting an unlimited population. The more of the original inhabitants that were slain, the more room would there be for the new settlers, and the better it would be for the Chosen Race.

The invasion was allowed to take the form of a punitive expedition. Those of us who have had experience of punitive expeditions, as on the North-West Frontier of India, know that on these occasions it becomes necessary to burn villages, destroy crops, food supplies and cattle, and to kill the adult male inhabitants. Such expeditions are carried out to avenge murders and similar lawlessness ; on the borders of civilization the threat of a punitive expedition forms the only argument by which lawlessness can be restrained. In this case however, the punishment was to be inflicted for transgressions against the laws of Jehovah, and to repress the practice of human sacrifice.

A modern, or mediæval, parallel is to be found in the conquest of Mexico. When the Spaniards landed, they were horrified to find that the inhabitants, though otherwise kind and gentle and in a comparatively advanced stage of civilization, extensively practised human sacrifice. Calling upon the name of the Virgin they outraged the altars and waged a relentless war against the inhabitants, whom they almost blotted out, and whose civilization they destroyed.

Some explanation still seems necessary as to why the massacres are said to have been carried out " as the Lord God of Israel commanded." In the contemporary records of the Egyptian and Asiatic conquerors, we generally find conquests effected and atrocities committed, with the approval of the nation's own particular gods. Now at this time Jehovah was regarded, not so much as the one Supreme Being, but rather as the tribal god of Israel, whose main delight was in their prosperity. What was for the good of Israel was pleasing to God ; what militated against the good of the community was displeasing to God. Can it be wondered at, then, that, just as the victories of the Egyptians and subsequent atrocities were believed by the Egyptians to be pleasing to the gods of Egypt, so the victories of the Israelites and subsequent atrocities were believed by the Israelites to be pleasing to the Lord God of Israel. Though we may not condone, we can at least understand the Israelites' belief that these massacres were acceptable to the Deity of their conception.

CHAPTER IV

THE JEWS

(WARS OF THE JUDGES AND KINGS)

THE wars with which we are next to deal scarcely amount to Conquests of Palestine. They consist rather of the local wars fought by the Jews between the dates of their settlement in, and expulsion from, the Holy Land. Nevertheless, they are so familiar that, without at least a passing reference, this book would be incomplete.

The wars that have been waged across the battlefields of Palestine may be roughly grouped into two categories; the great wars, in which the chief contestants and prizes lay far beyond the borders of the land, struggles between the empires of the Euphrates and of the Nile, into which the peoples of Palestine were unwillingly drawn owing to their geographical situation; and the merely local wars in which the sundry Palestinian tribes fought against one another or against their small aggressive neighbours. The wars dealt with in this chapter fall within the latter category.

One of the early oppressors of Israel was the Canaanitish king Jabin, whose capital was at Hazor, a few miles north-west of Lake Tiberias. At the instigation of the prophetess Deborah, Barak collected a sufficient force of the Israelites at Mount Tabor to oppose him. The hostile army of Jabin was strong in horses and chariots. Under his commander, Sisera, they were gathered upon the Plain of Esdraelon near the river Kishon. This is one of the few perennial rivers in Palestine;

it flows below the northern slopes of Carmel and reaches the sea at Haifa. As no rain falls in the summer, and the hosts of Sisera were swept away by the flood of the swollen river Kishon, it follows that the battle was fought in the rainy season. One who has experienced the quagmires of these Palestinian plains after heavy rain, can readily appreciate how the host of Sisera, with its horses and its chariots, must have fared, why it was thus overthrown by the hillmen of Barak's army, and why Sisera left his chariot and escaped on foot. The action of Jael, the wife of Heber the Kenite, fills us at first with amazement. But she was a Kenite, a wild half-savage tribeswoman from the Desert. Her conduct was on a par with that of the Mesopotamian Arabs of to-day, who hung about the battlefields to plunder, mutilate and murder the wounded, but always posed as friendly to the side which appeared to be winning. So, having first welcomed the vanquished Sisera to her tent, she slew him in his sleep, and thus sought to ingratiate herself with the victorious Israelites.

We next find the country overrun by the Midianites, wild hordes from the Desert, who are represented by the Bedouins of to-day. These swept over almost the whole land, pitching their tents and feeding their camels in the midst of the rich cornfields of Israel. The land lay uncultivated, while the people, faced with famine, fled to the mountain fastnesses and hid themselves in caves. Just as mysterious voices came to Joan of Arc calling upon her to go forth and deliver her country from its foreign oppressors, so did an angel appear to Gideon and commission him to deliver his country from its dire distress. The Midianites were encamped in the Vale of Jezreel, which is that portion of the Plain of Esdraelon that slopes down towards the Jordan. Gideon, having collected an army of Israelites, encamped upon the hills on the south side of the vale, the Midianite camp being thus below him in the valley. He selected three hundred of the bravest in his army for a night attack. Each man was provided with a trumpet and lantern, the light of the latter being concealed in an earthen pitcher. Silently at dead of night they crept down to the sleeping camp, undetected by the freshly posted sentries. Suddenly the trumpets blared, the pitchers crashed, the lanterns flashed out and the raiders shouted their war-cry. The panic in the Midianite camp was complete. The camels stampeded. The Midianites, with what discipline they may have ever possessed completely gone, and unable to distinguish friend from foe, killed one another in the dark. The camp broke up in hopeless confusion, and the frenzied fugitives fled towards their own country on the other side of the Jordan. Down the ravines poured the rabble seeking to make the fords of the river. Those that were not cut off at the fords were pursued into their own country, and a great host were slain, including Oreb and Zeb, Zeba and Salmanna. A most striking resemblance to this fleeing host was provided in September 1918, when the terrified Turks fled down these same ravines, into the hands of the British cavalry who were waiting to intercept them at the fords of the Jordan.

The exploits of Samson were not so much those of an army as of an individual. Strained relations must have existed then, as so frequently, between the Israelites in the hills and the Philistines upon the Plain. The Vale of Sorek, where he had an attraction in the person of Delilah, was the Wadi Surar, where now the railway passes, on its way from Junction Station up to Jerusalem. It was at Gaza that he was imprisoned, and from there that he removed the gates of the city " and carried them to the top of an hill, that is before Hebron." That hill, lying on the Hebron side of Gaza, is believed to be Ali Muntar, the commanding peak that overlooks the surrounding plain, and which played an important part in the operations of 1917. Having once escaped from Gaza, Samson foolishly allowed himself, through the medium of Delilah, to be betrayed into the hands of the Philistines. To Gaza, the chief city of the Philistines, he accordingly returned, and here, with eyes put out, and

THE JEWS (WARS OF THE JUDGES AND KINGS) 29

bound with brazen fetters, he was set the servile task of grinding at the prison mill. In Gaza it was, that, at last, with hair re-grown and strength restored, he brought down the temple of Dagon, perishing himself in the destruction that he accomplished.

The Israelites and the Philistines were constantly at war. Of such different extraction, it can be understood how it was that these races never blended. It is generally accepted that the Philistines had migrated from the isles of the Grecian archipelago. Their civilization and customs must have been European rather than Asiatic. The Jews, on the other hand, were Semitic. Differing thus in blood, in customs, and in creed, their estrangement must have been further emphasised by their relative geographical positions. The Philistines occupied the sea-board, with all the southern coastal towns. The caravan route to Egypt passed through Gaza, the principal town of Philistia. They held the keys of the trade routes from Judæa. But the Philistines held more than that. To them belonged the fertile plain, forming some of the richest corn land of Palestine, while the Israelites had to content themselves with the more barren mountains. When tribes of different race inhabit adjoining territories, the one rugged and mountainous and the other fertile and defenceless, the relationships existing are seldom amicable. The Philistines, like other foreigners, were despised by the Israelites and therefore by the authors of their historical works which have come down to us in the Bible. In point of fact, however, the civilization of the Philistines was probably in advance of that of Israel. In spite of the military disadvantages of their low-lying position for resistance against the hill tribes of Israel, we find that, not only did Israel never permanently annex Philistia, but that, on the other hand, the Philistines frequently gained the upper hand, carrying war into the country of the Israelites.

It was in one of these wars against the Philistines that the ark of the Lord was lost at the battle of Aphek, when Hophni and Phineas, the sons of Eli, were slain. The journeyings of that ark can easily be traced, for most of the towns at which it proved such a white elephant retain the same or similar names at the present day. No great stretch of the imagination is necessary to reproduce the scene, when, passing up the valley, by the present Junction Station, the two milch kine, drawing the new cart containing the ark, and lowing as they went, wended their way back into the country of the Israelites, to the spot where the people of Bethshemesh were harvesting their wheat in the valley.

The struggle between Church and State, which appears in the history of almost every nation, now appears in that of Israel. Hitherto the government of the loosely knit constituent tribes was administered by the hierarchy of the High Priesthood. The people of Israel, anxious to develop the military side of their national life, agitated for the severance of the civil from the religious administration and for the appointment of a sovereign. With none too good a grace Samuel conceded, and Saul was proclaimed king. The various tribes were now united under one autocratic ruler. Just as the Germans, after the binding together of the several Teutonic states into one consolidated empire, looked forward to a development upon military lines, so did the Israelites, by this political move, hope to achieve the military expansion of their little kingdom.

The expectations of the people were to some extent fulfilled. Saul entered upon a course of war in which his arms were at first attended with success. He conducted a successful expedition against the Amalekites, the wild people of the Southern Desert, when Agag, who walked "delicately," was captured and "hewn in pieces." But the warlike activities of Saul were mainly directed against the inveterate enemies, the Philistines. Most of these encounters probably took place in the foothills known as the Shephelah, between the highlands of Judæa and the Plain of Philistia, and it was here, no doubt, that

David in his boyhood slew the braggart champion of the Philistines, Goliath.

It was on the Plain of Esdraelon, however, that the greatest of these battles was fought between the Israelites and the Philistines. That the battle should have been fought there, so far north of the normal boundaries of the Philistines' territory, shows the great extent of their conquests, involving the subjugation of the whole southern realm. The Philistines were gathered together at Aphek, on the Plain of Esdraelon; the Israelites by the valley of Jezreel. The Israelites were routed and fled towards Mount Gilboa, the mountain which closes in the plain upon the south-east. As they fled up the hill side they were pursued by the arrows of the Philistines. Saul himself was wounded by one such arrow, whereupon he put himself out of his misery. The Israelite inhabitants fled from all the neighbouring towns. The Philistines took the body of Saul and fastened it to the wall of Beth-shan, the modern Beisan, which stands at the junction of the Vale of Jezreel and the Jordan valley.

David followed Saul upon the throne of Israel. Although the Israelites had been in Palestine for three or four centuries when he succeeded to the throne, there were certain individual cities that still remained in the possession of the Canaanite tribes. One such city was the strongly posted hill fortress of Jebus or Jerusalem, in the possession of the Jebusites. It was David who captured Jerusalem and removed thither his capital from Hebron; hence Jerusalem is spoken of as the " City of David." His reign was full of wars, in the course of which his dominions were extended from the River of Egypt (the Wadi el Arish) as far as the banks of the Euphrates. This was the greatest extent ever attained by the kingdom of the Hebrews, and was quite small in comparison with the empires of its mighty neighbours. In the course of these wars David defeated amongst others the Philistines, whose yoke he removed from Israel, the Syrians of Damascus, and the smaller tribes occupying the territories skirting the Desert. It was during one of these latter wars, fought against the Ammonites, possibly near the modern Amman, that Uriah the Hittite was placed in the forefront that he might be slain in battle.

David was followed by Solomon, whose reign was a reign of peace and commercial prosperity. Entering into alliances with the Phœnicians and the Egyptians, and with his territories extending to the Mediterranean, the Red Sea and the Euphrates, he was able to establish a considerable mercantile carrying trade. Most of the great trade routes of Western Asia now passed through his dominions. Is it surprising that great wealth was amassed.

Among Solomon's seven hundred wives, the chief seems to have been an Egyptian princess, a daughter of Pharaoh. Nevertheless, it was not a child by this wife that succeeded him on the throne, but his son Rehoboam. This king proved himself an unwise and headstrong ruler, threatening to dragoon his subjects in a manner which drove ten of the twelve tribes into instant revolt under Jeroboam. Shishak, the King of Egypt, now led an invading army into Palestine in support of Jeroboam. This expedition may have been dictated from motives of jealousy because a son of Solomon by Pharaoh's daughter had not succeeded him on the throne. Or it may be that Shishak, who was the first king of a new Egyptian dynasty, was wholly out of sympathy with Solomon and his descendants. Whatever the motive may have been, we know that Shishak came up out of Egypt, with a great army against Judah and that Rehoboam discreetly submitted, buying off the invader with treasures from the temple. This invasion under Shishak is from the antiquarian's point of view most interesting. Upon the wall of the great temple at Karnak (Luxor) are inscribed, not only the names of all the cities that Shishak overthrew, but also portraits depicting the type of men who then inhabited the country. From these it appears that the prevalent type

THE JEWS (WARS OF THE JUDGES AND KINGS)

in Southern Palestine was still the Amorite; that the indigenous Canaanitish type had been by no means obliterated.

The capital of the northern kingdom of Israel was established at Samaria, three or four miles from the modern Nablous. This kingdom found itself in frequent conflict with its northern neighbours, the Syrians, whose capital was at Damascus. These were the wars in which so prominent a part was played by the prophet Elisha. From Damascus to Samaria came the Syrian commander, Naaman, to be healed by Elisha of his leprosy, when to his intense disgust he was told to go and wash in the Jordan. Elisha's continuous advice to the king of Israel in these wars was so invaluable that not once nor twice did the Israelites avoid ambushes laid by the Syrians, owing to the prophet's timely warning. Determined to put a stop to this, the king of Syria despatched a force to cut off Elisha at Dothan. But, smitten with blindness, the force was led away by Elisha until they found themselves in Samaria, the capital of Israel, and were delivered into the hands of the Israelite king. The most terrible event in these wars was the dreadful siege of Samaria in which the citizens were reduced to the most loathsome of food. The siege was raised miraculously. The Syrians were seized with a panic in the night and stampeded. They had heard a false rumour that the Egyptians or possibly the Hittites, both mighty peoples, were again coming to the aid of the Israelites. Though the Israelites feared the Syrians, yet much more did the Syrians fear the powerful Hittites and Egyptians.

The civil war and the usurpation of Jehu form a gruesome melodrama in the history of Israel. The opening scenes were enacted upon the Plain of Esdraelon and the valley of Jezreel. The Israelite king, wounded in the wars against the Syrians, was convalescing at Jezreel, when Jehu came, driving furiously. Furiously did he drive, not only his chariot but also his revolution. From Jezreel he passed on to Samaria, putting the king's relatives to death with a ruthlessness that almost excelled that of mediæval Italy or modern Turkey.

The kingdoms of Judah and Israel had no prolonged period of liberty still ahead. The rising tide of Assyria was soon to sweep away Israel, while her successor was to lead the sister kingdom of Judah into captivity by the waters of Babylon.

CHAPTER V

THE ASSYRIANS AND BABYLONIANS

A BUFFER State, between the mighty empires of the Euphrates and the Nile, is the position which Palestine occupied throughout ancient history. The importance of Jerusalem, as the city of God, figures so largely in the pages of the Biblical narrative, that we are tempted to overlook the insignificance which this country really possessed in comparison with her mighty neighbours. In no portion of its history is this feature more clearly emphasised than in the struggles from the eighth to the sixth centuries before Christ, culminating in the Jewish exile to Babylon.

When one speaks of a buffer state at the present day, one instinctively looks for a parallel in the Low Countries of Europe, particularly Belgium. The analogy between the position of Belgium in the present century and that of Samaria in the eighth century B.C. is sufficiently close to assist our understanding of the Biblical position at this period. Belgium, situated between the great military powers of France and Germany, has been so frequently fought over as to have acquired the name of " the cockpit of Europe." In 1914 it lay directly in the line of advance which Germany considered necessary for her invasion of France. So Belgium had for a time to submit to invasion and annexation. Holland, on the other hand, lay off the main German line of advance, but its position throughout the great war was one of extreme peril. The possession of that country, commanding the mouths of the

Rhine, though not immediately necessary to Germany, would nevertheless have been of material advantage, and essential to her ultimate development. There can be little doubt that, had Germany proved successful, the absorption of Belgium into the German Empire would have been immediate, and that of Holland, at a later date, inevitable.

Let us apply the analogy to the position of Palestine in the eighth century B.C. The normal road from Assyria into Egypt ran then, as it does now, through Damascus and along the plain of Esdraelon, crossing, near Samaria, the low mountains which join Carmel with the main range of Southern Palestine. It then passed southward down the coastal plain, through Philistia, by the frontier towns of Gaza and Lachish and so across the Desert to Egypt. Thus Jerusalem and Judæa, perched on their hills, lay off the direct road, which they merely threatened but did not obstruct. To an Assyrian army, wishing to maintain its communications with Egypt, the possession of Samaria was thus indispensable, the annexation of Jerusalem and Judæa, merely desirable. So there was not the same urgency for the capture of Jerusalem as there was for the capture of Samaria ; the conquest of Jerusalem might well be left for a more convenient season. Thus we find Jerusalem and Judæa continuing their independence in spite of the rising tide of Assyria, and outliving the independence of her sister kingdom of Samaria by more than a century.

The first introduction of the Assyrians was on the invitation of the Jews themselves. Pekah, King of Israel, entered into a confederacy with Rezin, King of Damascus, to invade Judæa, and Judæa was defeated. The Edomites and Philistines revolted. Ahaz, King of Judæa, thus attacked on all sides, threw himself in his desperation under the protection of Tiglath-Pileser, King of Assyria. The Assyrian lent his aid as far as suited his own views of conquest, invaded Syria, took Damascus, slew their king, and, according to the custom of the Assyrians, led the people away into captivity. But against the more immediate enemies of Ahaz, the Edomites, he sent no help, but merely laid the kingdom of Judah under tribute.

A colony of Assyrians having been planted in Damascus, the borders of Assyria now marched with those of Israel. Very soon we find Shalmaneser, King of Assyria, making an expedition against Hoshea, King of Israel, bringing that country to submission, and placing it under tribute. Hoshea entered upon intrigues with the King of Egypt, seeking his assistance to throw off the Assyrian yoke. Throughout this history, we find the dealings of the Palestinian nations with Egypt singularly unfortunate. In so far as military assistance was concerned, Egypt seems to have been wholly unreliable and to have fully deserved the subsequent taunt of Rabshakeh, "this bruised reed, Egypt, on which, if a man lean, it will go into his hand, and pierce it." Shalmaneser made an expedition against Samaria, which he captured after a siege lasting for three years. During so long a siege there must have been ample opportunity for the Egyptians to come to the relief of Samaria, had they been willing and able to do so. Probably Samaria was encouraged to prolong its resistance by the hope that Egypt would send an army and raise the siege. But Egypt appears to have done nothing, and Samaria fell in the year 722 B.C. The inhabitants, not only of the cities, but of the country districts as well, were evacuated to Media and Persia at the extreme opposite end of the Assyrian Empire, while their places were taken by other colonists from those distant countries. These immigrant colonists, Cutheans, were the progenitors of the much despised "Samaritans" of the New Testament. The former inhabitants, expelled into the heart of Asia, disappear from history; though not from imagination, however, for the "lost ten tribes" are traced by some in the Semitic-looking Afghans, and, more fancifully, by others in the Red Indians of North America.

At this stage of the operations, Sennacherib appears upon the scene. Succeeding to the throne of Assyria shortly after the capture of Samaria, we soon find him on the war-path against Judah. Reigning at Jerusalem at this time was Hezekiah, an able monarch, combining prudence and wisdom with piety and modesty, virtues none too common among Eastern potentates. Aided by the advice of Isaiah, he successfully steered his kingdom through crises of great gravity. Seven years after the fall of Samaria, Sennacherib made an expedition against Judah, with a great army. Hezekiah had refused to pay the tribute to Assyria, which had been formerly paid by his father, Ahaz. Presumably making this a pretext, Sennacherib took all the cities of Judah by force; but when he was ready to bring his army against Jerusalem, Hezekiah surrendered at discretion. The tribute which Hezekiah was forced to pay was large, in so much that the treasures had to be taken from the royal palace and from the temple; but there is little doubt that, had Jerusalem then held out against the whole host of Assyria, it would have been taken and looted, and the inhabitants carried off into captivity. Hezekiah was probably wise in his discretion.

Sennacherib now turned his eyes towards that much more attractive prize, Egypt. He marched with his main army down the maritime plain, overrunning Philistia, until he reached the city of Lachish. This place has been identified with Tel-el-Hesi in the Wadi-Hesi a few miles to the east or north-east of Gaza. Here it formed an obstacle across his path, which must be removed before the road would be open to Egypt. Accordingly he embarked upon operations for its capture. In the meanwhile, somewhat as a side-show, he also turned his attention towards Jerusalem. Although Sennacherib had previously allowed himself to be bought off by Hezekiah with an enormous tribute, yet he had no compunction in now again attempting the capture of Jerusalem, if that could be effected without any great expenditure of military resource. Accordingly he tried bluff. From Lachish, where he was warring against the Egyptians, or their Philistine allies, he sent a military

THE ASSYRIANS AND BABYLONIANS

deputation up into the hills to demand the surrender of Jerusalem. The arrogant speech of his emissaries is too well known to need repetition. Hezekiah's position was critical. He had already denuded himself and his city of all its treasure, but in vain ; so it was useless for him to think again of purchasing peace by payment. On the other hand the position of Sennacherib was now very different from that on the previous occasion. Then the whole army of Assyria was directed against Jerusalem, and the main object was plunder. Now the bulk of the Assyrian army was directed against Lachish and the Egyptians ; while Jerusalem was no longer worth plundering. Its capture was advantageous, but by no means essential, to the invasion of Egypt ; Hezekiah conferred with Isaiah and wisely refused to surrender the city.

The messengers of Sennacherib returned from the Judæan hills to the Plain. During their absence Sennacherib had captured Lachish and had probably moved forward across the Desert to Libnah or Pelusium. Pelusium was at the mouth of a branch of the Nile, long since dried up, which in those days flowed into the sea to the east of Port Said. Pelusium was therefore on the extreme east of the Delta and must then have formed the key of Egypt.

At this time the chief power to be reckoned with in the Valley of the Nile was, not the King of Egypt properly so called, but the King of Ethiopia, that is, of the Soudan. When Sennacherib heard that the King of Ethiopia had come out to fight against him, he redoubled his efforts to cow Jerusalem into surrender. He sent another and yet more blasphemous letter to Hezekiah, which the latter treated with befitting piety and humility, spreading the letter before the Lord. Then, still following the counsel of Isaiah, he returned a firm refusal to the swashbuckling messengers of the King of Assyria. A terrible catastrophe overwhelmed the army of Sennacherib. Whatever may have actually happened, it is clear that the army was destroyed, not by defeat in battle at the hand of man, but by some natural or miraculous cause which we should designate an " Act of God." At this time the bulk of the Assyrian force was probably at Pelusium, with a smaller force outside Jerusalem. Where the disaster occurred is not certain. According to Josephus it was outside the Walls of Jerusalem. The Egyptian records, on the other hand, speak of some such deliverance occurring near their borders, which they naturally ascribe to their own gods. On the whole, modern opinion inclines towards the host having been overwhelmed by a pestilence at Pelusium or in the desert. Here the host may easily have been assailed by some disease from the Delta, with the result so graphically described.[1] It seems reasonable to suppose that it was the main army that was thus assailed, and that such main army was warring against Egypt and not merely lying round the walls of Jerusalem. Whether the disaster was due, as some suppose, to a simoon, or as Josephus states, to a pestilence, it is clear that the Assyrians had received such a blow that Sennacherib withdrew from the neighbourhood of Egypt; and that for the remainder of his reign, the armies of the Assyrians troubled Palestine no more.

Esarhaddon succeeded his father Sennacherib on the throne of Assyria. Twenty-nine years after the disaster that befell his father's army, we find him directing the Assyrian army once more against Egypt. On this occasion Jerusalem offered no resistance and the reigning king, Manasseh, was carried off into captivity at Babylon. Tehrak of Ethiopia, the adversary of Sennacherib, was still king of Egypt and the Nile Valley. He took up a defensive position at Pelusium, prepared to bar the advance of the Assyrian army along the coastal route to Egypt. Esarhaddon prevailed upon the Arab sheikhs of the desert to lend their aid, by conveying the water necessary for the use of the army in skins on the backs of camels, and struck southwards through the waste tract known as the Desert of Shur. By this manœuvre he turned the flank of the Egyptian

[1] 2 Kings xix. 35.

army and gained the fertile country of Egypt. A great battle was fought, in which the Assyrians prevailed, while Tehrak's forces were driven from the field in confusion. Pushing forward up the valley of the Nile, the Assyrians made themselves masters of all Egypt, from the Mediterranean to the First Cataract. The Egyptians refused passively to submit to the domination of the Assyrians, and, after successive struggles, which belong rather to the history of Egypt than of Palestine, the Assyrians withdrew.

Then occurred that change in the condition of affairs on the Euphrates, which resulted in the supersession of the Assyrians by the Babylonians. In the interval, the Egyptians revived, and, under Pharaoh Necho, turned their eyes again towards the Euphrates.

It mattered little which way the tide of conquest flowed. The intervening kingdom of Judah suffered alike, whether it flowed towards Egypt or towards Babylon. Josiah, the King of Judah, was now bound to the Assyrian interest by the terms of his vassalage, by treaty, and by gratitude for the permission to extend his sovereignty over Samaria. In 608 B.C. Pharaoh Necho determined to invade Asia. At the head of a large army he took the coast route into Syria, supported by his Mediterranean fleet along the shore, and, proceeding through the low tracts of Philistia and Sharon, prepared to cross the ridge of hills which separates the Plain of Sharon from the Plain of Esdraelon. Here he found his passage barred by the army of Josiah, who, resolved to oppose the further progress of the Egyptians, had occupied a strong position near Megiddo, on the southern verge of the Plain of Esdraelon. Necho endeavoured to dissuade Josiah from his rash enterprise, but in vain. A battle was fought, in which the Jewish army suffered complete defeat. Josiah was killed, while the triumphant Necho pushed onward through Syria, carrying all before him, as far as Carchemish on the Euphrates. Judah now became tributary to Egypt.

The alternate supremacy of Egypt and Babylon must have been most uncomfortable for the unfortunate people of Palestine, ground as it were, between two millstones. Rapid was the rise of Babylonia on the ruins of Assyria, and in the year 601 B.C. Nebuchadnezzar, having retaken Carchemish, passed the Euphrates and soon overran the whole of Syria and Palestine. The unfortunate Judah, scarce recovered from the punishment which it received from Egypt for its adherence to Babylon, was now punished again by Babylon for its adherence to Egypt. Jerusalem made little resistance, and Jehoiakim the king and many of the nobles were carried away to Babylon. It is from this year (607 B.C.) that the seventy years of the captivity are reckoned. Jehoiakim was afterwards reinstated upon his throne at Jerusalem as a vassal of Babylon. But after three years he foolishly attempted to throw off that yoke. On the arrival of Nebuchadnezzar the city surrendered at discretion, and most of the remaining nobles and treasures were carried off to Babylon. Zedekiah was allowed to reign over such kingdom as was left. Even he could not let sleeping dogs lie, but allowed himself to be beguiled into making a treaty with Egypt for the purpose of again opposing Babylon. This was too much for Nebuchadnezzar's patience. He came once more against Jerusalem. The Egyptians despatched a relief expedition into Palestine, which only recoiled before Babylon, and Zedekiah was left to himself. In 586 B.C. Jerusalem fell, Zedekiah was made a prisoner and deprived of his sight, while the Temple and city were burnt and the bulk of the people carried into captivity.

Thus the last of the buffer States between the Empires of the Euphrates and of the Nile had gone. The empires had now become conterminous, and a few years later Nebuchadnezzar overran Egypt.

The contrast between the exile of the Northern and Southern kingdoms is thus summed up by Josephus:—

" Such was the end of the nation of the Hebrews, as it hath been delivered down to us, it having twice gone beyond Euphrates. For the people of the ten tribes were carried out of Samaria by the Assyrians in the days of king Hoshea. After which the people of the two tribes that remained, after Jerusalem was taken, were carried away by Nebuchadnezzar, the king of Babylon and Chaldea. Now as to Shalmanezer, he removed the Israelites out of their country, and placed therein the nation of the Cutheans, who had formerly belonged to the inner parts of Persia and Media, but were then called Samaritans, by taking the name of the country to which they were removed. But the king of Babylon, who brought out the two tribes, placed no other nation in their country, by which means all Judæa and Jerusalem and the temple continued to be a desert for seventy years."

CHAPTER VI

THE GREEKS

THE restoration of Jerusalem was consequent upon the overthrow of Babylonia by the Medes and Persians. Cyrus the Persian, influenced by considerations of political wisdom or religious toleration, gave permission to as many of the exiles as wished to do so to return to their beloved city of Jerusalem. We have seen that the Babylonians, while carrying the inhabitants of the city into exile, had not implanted foreign colonists in the neighbourhood of Jerusalem. Doubtless the country people had been allowed to remain on the land, and these must have welcomed the returning exiles. Although the latter found the city a desolate waste, yet, with the aid of the country people, they reconstructed a Jewish State. In spite of determined hostility from the Cuthites or Samaritans, the temple was rebuilt in 537 B.C. under Zerubbabel. Jerusalem had lain waste for about half a century.

That at this time so little part in the contemporary history of the country was played by Jerusalem must have been due to the miserable state of insignificance to which it had been reduced through its destruction at the hands of the Babylonians, and not to the absence of stirring events in the country. Cambyses, who succeeded his father Cyrus in 529 B.C., soon set about the reduction of Egypt. He first secured the adhesion of the Phœnician cities; then, with their aid, he detached Cyprus from her Egyptian masters; and finally, with the aid of Phœnician, Cypriote and Greek ships, he proceeded against Egypt both by land and sea. He marched his army across the desert, following the example of Esarhaddon, and making an alliance with a Bedouin sheik for the transportation of the necessary water on camels. A battle was fought at Pelusium, and the Egyptians were completely defeated and fled to Memphis (Cairo). This city was blockaded both by land and river and fell to Cambyses. He then overran Egypt, destroying and mutilating beautiful monuments, which, to this day, show traces of his iconoclasm; the destruction of the thousand-ton statue of Rameses at Thebes, now lying fallen and shattered, forms a lasting memorial of his handiwork.

We read of the opposition which the Jews encountered in their attempt to rebuild Jerusalem, and how their neighbours represented to Cambyses (Artaxerxes) that this city had been a seditious city and had for this reason been destroyed; thus they persuaded him to forbid the restoration. Picture Cambyses at the time as operating in Egypt, with his line of communications through Palestine. Jerusalem would have appeared to him much as it did to Nebuchadnezzar; that is, as a potential danger to his line of communications. In prohibiting the reconstruction of the city and temple he probably thought far more of the possible military effect of the city being rebuilt, than of the national and religious aspirations of the Jews for the restoration of their temple.

After the death of Cambyses, the embargo on building at Jerusalem was removed, and the reconstruction of the city, and more especially of the temple, was resumed under Zerubbabel. The High Priest at this time filled the position of chief authority in Jerusalem, and was the person responsible to the Persian king for the government of the city and surrounding district. Matters seem to have gone on quietly at Jerusalem under the new regime for about sixty years. Then there was a further emigration of Jews from Babylon under the leadership of Ezra, while a few years later, in 445 B.C., Nehemiah came to

Jerusalem and inaugurated a thorough scheme of reconstruction.

The westward progress of the Persians in Europe met with far less success than in Africa. Upon the very threshold of that continent they were held up by the Greeks. Marathon, Thermopylæ, Salamis are household words. The power of little Greece, which mighty Persia had once disdained, subsequently rebounded with a force capable of overthrowing the Persian empire and of Europeanising the whole of the Middle East. Hitherto the tides of conquest that have surged across Palestine have been those of Asia and Africa. Henceforth Africa becomes a negligible quantity and is superseded in importance by Europe.

A century and a half had elapsed since the check of the Persians at Marathon, when Alexander embarked upon his great campaign. It was in 334 B.C. that he crossed the Hellespont and fought his first battle against the Persian satraps at the Granicus in Asia Minor. Alexander did not yet possess the command of the sea, and the whole coast of Asia Minor was subject to Persia. Had he pushed at once right into the heart of Asia, he would have left it possible for the admiral, who commanded for Darius the Persian king on this coast, to have raised all Asia Minor against him or transferred the war back to Macedonia. Accordingly Alexander turned south to subdue first the coasts of the Persian empire, thus neutralising the hostile country which would be left in his rear, and rendering harmless the enemy fleet based thereon. Having captured Sardis, the key of the high roads eastward, and Halicarnassus, he felt free to press on and strike at the headquarters of the enemies' power, Phœnicia. Accordingly he crossed the Taurus mountains and occupied Cilicia. The Persian king was awaiting him with a large army in the plain of Syria near Damascus. But the Persian king unwisely left this favourable position, moved to the north of Syria, and reached the rear of Alexander's army at Issus near the head of the Gulf of Alex-

THE GREEKS

andretta. Here the Persians took up a position behind the army of Alexander, cutting him off from his communications with Greece, and compelling him to fight. At this point the mountains approach very close to the sea; here, on this narrow intervening neck of land, was fought the decisive battle of Issus. The Persians were completely defeated and Alexander was left free for another forward move.

Alexander marched southwards. Moving along the coast, he besieged, captured and destroyed Tyre, the stronghold of the Phœnicians. Continuing his march, he captured and totally destroyed Gaza. While he was at the siege of Tyre, Alexander sent thence to demand the surrender of Jerusalem. The High Priest answered that he had sworn fealty to Darius, and was bound to maintain allegiance to that monarch. When, however, after the destruction of Gaza, Alexander advanced against Jerusalem, the High Priest and people discreetly changed their attitude. Wise in their generation, they threw open their gates and extended a welcome to Alexander. Doubtless they knew better than once more to incur the penalties of buttressing the declining fortunes of a distant and decadent suzerain.

Alexander moved down into Egypt. Here he delayed for a short while, regulating the country as a province under his sway, with kindness towards the inhabitants and respect for their religion. On the further side of the Delta, beyond the alluvial mud of the Nile, where the firm rocky strata reach the sea, he established a port and founded the city of Alexandria. He had thus mastered the whole littoral of the Eastern Mediterranean, and was in a position to turn his eyes further Eastward towards the heart of the Persian Empire. He returned through Syria past Damascus, crossed the Euphrates, marched over the Plains of Mesopotamia and across the Tigris to beyond Nineveh (Mosul). He eventually met, and finally defeated, the Persian army at the battle of Arbela. We need not follow his fortunes further as he marched eastward into India, conquering and carrying all before him as he went, until, on the Plains of the Punjab, his soldiers refused to go further, and he was compelled to turn his face again towards the west. He was only thirty-two years of age when death overtook him at Babylon; his career had been short, brilliant, meteoric.

A permanent result of Alexander's sweep, so far as Palestine and the adjoining countries were concerned, was, that he changed the character of the government from Asiatic to European, from Persian to Greek. On Alexander's death in 323 B.C. his empire split up into independent Grecian kingdoms. Palestine did not escape the dreadful anarchy which ensued during the destructive warfare waged by his generals and successors. Twice the provinces of Syria and Judæa fell into the power of Antigonus, and twice were regained by Ptolemy, to whose share they were finally adjudged after the decisive defeat of Antigonus at Ipsus. The maritime towns, Tyre, Joppa and Gaza were the chief objects of contention; Jerusalem itself seems to have escaped the horrors of war.

The founding of the Syro-Grecian kingdom by Seleucus, and the establishment of Antioch as the capital, brought Judæa once more into the unfortunate situation of a weak province, placed between two great conflicting monarchies. Syria, instead of a satrapy of the great but remote Persian empire, became a powerful kingdom, ruled by ambitious princes, while Antioch became one of the most flourishing cities in the world. The Seleucidan kingdom in Northern Syria could not but come into constant collision with the Ptolemaic kingdom in Egypt; and Jerusalem seemed doomed to be among the prizes of this interminable warfare and in turn vassal to each.

Throughout this period of Grecian ascendancy, the history of Judæa bears a resemblance to that of modern Serbia. During the last decade we have seen Serbia embroiled in two royal assassinations, the one terminating a dynasty and the other deluging Europe in blood; we have seen her exploited in turn by her powerful neighbours; we have seen her taking an active,

THE GREEKS

if unwilling, part in no less than three distinct wars; we have seen her territory occupied by a savage and relentless foe, her people crushed, and her army driven beyond her borders; and now at last we have seen the wheel of fortune restore her again to independence. In the same way the history of Judæa, at the period which we are considering, presents an interminable kaleidoscope of intrigues, murders, usurpations, invasions and conquests; wars of oppression and wars of liberation; subjection to Egypt and subjection to Antioch; in such a manner that any attempt to follow the thread of the story is bewildering.

We will not attempt therefore to follow this period in detail but content ourselves with a passing glance at some of the more picturesque or stirring incidents.

About 321 B.C. Ptolemy, the King of Egypt, attempted to seize the whole of Syria. Advancing against Jerusalem, he assaulted it on the Sabbath, and met with no resistance, because the superstitious Jews scrupled to violate the holy day even in self-defence. He carried away with him into Egypt a large number of captives, who formed the nucleus of the Jewish colony that has long existed, and is found to this day, in Alexandria.

It was not, however, the tyranny of foreign sovereigns, but the jealous rivalry of her native rulers that precipitated the calamities that befel the holy city. Antiochus Epiphanes had succeeded to the throne of Syria. Courted by rival claimants to the High Priesthood at Jerusalem, he dispossessed one, Jason, and appointed his brother Menelaus to be High Priest. In the year 169 B.C. Antiochus had advanced into Egypt and conquered that country. Unfortunately a false rumour of his death reached Jerusalem, and Jason, the dispossessed High Priest, seized the opportunity of revolt against his brother, took the city, imprisoned Menelaus and began to exercise a terrible vengeance against the opposite party. The intelligence of the insurrection, magnified into a deliberate revolt of the whole nation, reached Antiochus. He came up against Jerusalem on his return from Egypt and overthrew the city. He slew a large number of the inhabitants, and pillaged the temple. In his zeal for the religion of the Greeks, or his detestation of that of the Hebrews, he adopted every conceivable measure to defile the temple and suppress the Hebrew religion. He forbade the Jews to offer the accustomed daily sacrifices. Some of the inhabitants he slew, and some he carried away captive, together with their wives and children to the number of about ten thousand. He built an idol altar upon God's altar and slew swine upon it, thus defiling the sanctuary with the most odious form of sacrilege conceivable in the eyes of the Jews. He compelled them to forsake the worship of their own God, and made them build temples, and raise idol altars, in every city and village, and offer swine upon them daily. Books of the law when found were all destroyed. He tried to stop the practice of circumcision. Those who resisted the persecution and clung to their religion were whipped with rods; their bodies were torn to pieces and crucified while they were still alive. Such women as had their sons circumcised, these did his myrmidons strangle with their sons, hanging the sons about the necks of the mothers as they were upon the crosses.

The darkest hour is just before the dawn. The black night of persecution under Antiochus Epiphanes was to end in the dawn of the heroic age under the Maccabees. The extravagant excesses of Antiochus Epiphanes produced a revolution. Mattathias the father of five sons, the Maccabees, slew the king's emissary and summoned all the citizens who were zealous for the Jewish law to follow him to the mountains. In these mountain fastnesses, adherents rapidly swelled their numbers. A thousand of them were surprised in a cave and attacked; as it was the Sabbath day, they offered no resistance and were slain to a man. Thenceforth this extreme and superstitious observance of the Sabbath was so far modified as to permit of defensive, but still not of offensive, warfare on that day. Concealing themselves in their mountain fastnesses, these insurgents raided the towns and villages as opportunity offered, destroying the heathen altars, enforcing circumcision, and punishing all apostates who fell into their hands.

On the death of Mattathias the command passed to his son Judas Maccabeus, whose name, magnified in song, has come down to us as that of the Conquering Hero. Having tried his soldiers with many gallant adventures, Judas determined to meet the enemy in the field. He first defeated and slew the Governor of Samaria. Then the Deputy-Governor of Cœle-syria (Northern Syria), advancing to revenge this defeat, was encountered in the pass of Beth-horon, and met the same fate. The rapid progress of Judas demanded immediate resistance. A Syrian army, amounting to forty thousand foot and seven thousand horse, advanced rapidly into the province. With them came a multitude of slave-merchants for the purpose of taking the insurgents captive and selling them as slaves for the benefit of the Syrian king's finances. Judas assembled his force at Mizpeh, probably the mountain Neby Samwil, the key of Jerusalem. His small force consisted of some three thousand men, ill-armed, but fired with patriotic and religious enthusiasm. From Mizpeh he moved down towards Emmaus, where the enemy lay encamped. A portion of the enemy army having been detached to surprise him by night, Judas eluded them and fell upon their camp in their absence. The fight that followed was short, sharp and decisive. The camp was captured, and when the Syrians returned from their weary and fruitless search through the mountains they found their camp in flames. The Syrians fled without striking a blow and much booty fell into the hands of Judas and his followers. With just retribution, many of the slave-merchants were themselves sold for slaves. Judas then crossed the Jordan, met and defeated another Syrian force that was there collecting against him, and brought to a close the first triumphant campaign of the Maccabees.

Campaign followed campaign, until eventually Judas had thrown off the Syrian yoke, established himself in Jerusalem, and purified and restored the temple. The Syrians and their allies, discomfited on every side, began to revenge themselves on the Jews who were scattered in Galilee and the provinces beyond the Jordan. Judas conducted punitive expeditions into these provinces. The Maccabees were irresistible.

Further expeditions were sent against Judas in the reigns of succeeding kings of Syria, but after varying fortunes Judas still emerged victorious. At length he took a more decided step to secure the independence of his country and entered into a treaty with Rome. But before this treaty was made known the glorious career of Judas had terminated. Deserted by his troops, Judas refused to retreat before another army of the Syrian king, but fell, as he had lived, the champion of his country's liberty.

Judas Maccabeus was succeeded by his brother Jonathan, who fell, after a varying, warlike, but on the whole successful career of some seventeen years, and was succeeded by his brother Simon, the last of the Maccabees.

We cannot attempt a complete or detailed history of the Holy Land. So we must pass over the century of plot, counter plot, and war that followed the death of the last of the Maccabees. The independence so bravely won by the Maccabees was sustained; and, throughout this period, instead of foreign wars, the strife and bloodshed centred round the quarrels of the rival Jewish factions at home. It was during such quarrels as these between the brothers Aristobolus and Hyrcanus, over the succession to the throne, that the curtain descended upon what we have regarded as the Greek period, to rise again upon that of Rome.

CHAPTER VII

THE ROMANS

SEVENTY years before the birth of Our Lord, the rival claimants to the independent throne of Jerusalem were the two brothers Hyrcanus and Aristobulus. At first these brothers were prepared to share the honours amicably, Aristobulus being King, and Hyrcanus contenting himself with the office of High Priest. Over-persuaded, however, by his friends, especially by one Antipater, the father of Herod (afterwards Herod the Great), Hyrcanus fled to the Arabian capital of Petra, and stirred up the Arabians against his brother. War ensued between the Arabians and Aristobulus, in which the Arabians were at first successful; but they subsequently withdrew on receiving peremptory orders to do so from Rome.

The mighty empire of Rome was already commencing to overshadow Western Asia. Pompey, who had been warring in Armenia, passed over into Syria and came to Damascus. Here he was appealed to, both by Aristobulus and by Hyrcanus. Pompey heard the causes of the rival brothers, speaking civilly to them both, and promising to settle all their affairs upon his return. He then moved on into Arabia, for the reduction of that country and of its capital Petra. On his return into Syria, Pompey marched through Jericho into Judæa, espousing the cause of Hyrcanus. Aristobulus, on the other hand, had meanwhile endeavoured to put the country in a state of defence, and had shut himself up in a strong citadel on a rock called Alexandrion. Forced by Pompey to do so, Aristobulus here signed written orders to all his fortresses to surrender, but himself fled to Jerusalem, where he prepared for resistance.

As Pompey approached the city, Aristobulus came out to meet him and offered to surrender upon terms. Pompey accepted the surrender. But, when those of the Roman army, whom he had sent forward to enter the city, reached the gates, they were refused admission. The bolder of the adherents of Aristobulus within the city had meantime got the upper hand, closed the gates, and manned the walls. Enraged at this action, Pompey threw Aristobulus into prison, and came himself to the city. Inside the walls there was dissension. The adherents of Aristobulus were for offering a stout resistance; those of Hyrcanus, for admitting the Romans. Eventually the party of Hyrcanus opened the gates and admitted the Romans to the city; but the party of Aristobulus took possession of the Temple, and, putting it into a state of defence, offered a determined resistance. Here they were rigorously besieged for a period of three months. The Romans piled up banks and filled up the ditch, and brought up war engines and battering rams from Tyre. The Jews, in their superstitious devotion to the observance of the Sabbath, refused to take any except defensive action upon that day. Accordingly the Romans, when they realized this, abstained from offensive action on the Sabbath, and took advantage of the day to improve their earthworks and to bring their engines of war into position unmolested. Eventually one of the towers of defence was battered down; the Romans mounted the breach; the temple had been captured. And now all was full of slaughter, some of the Jews being slain by the Romans and some by one another, while some of them even threw themselves down the precipices. Pompey entered the temple and to the horror of the Jews saw " all that which it was unlawful for any other man to see, but only for the High Priests." All the riches of the temple he left untouched, only to be plundered a few years later by the avaricious Crassus. The temple area he ordered to be purified. Hyrcanus he restored to the high priesthood, but without the royal dignity; Aristobulus he removed to Rome. Jerusalem became tributary to Rome 63 B.C.

During the great civil war the fate of Judæa, like that of the world, hung in the balance. When the star of Julius Cæsar was in the ascendant Hyrcanus and Antipater were advanced to power. The latter was appointed Procurator over the whole of Judæa, and his son Herod was appointed to the government of Galilee. Herod now stands out as the foremost character in the history of Judæa. Hard and cruel beyond description, he was nevertheless so skilful a trimmer, that he not only retained his authority, but continued to advance in power, whichever party was in the ascendant at Rome. After the death of Cæsar he insinuated himself into the favour of Cassius. Then, when the fate of the world was decided at Philippi, he hastened to render his allegiance to Mark Antony. On the death of Antipater, Herod and his brother were appointed Tetrarchs of Judæa.

But now the Parthians, sweeping westward from Central Asia, entered Syria and Asia Minor, and overran the whole region. They plundered Jerusalem and ravaged the country. Herod fled to Rome. Here he prospered beyond his highest expectations. Augustus and Antony united in conferring upon him the crown of Judæa. He hastened back, speedily raised a force, united with some Roman auxiliaries, took Joppa, overran Galilee, and sat down before Jerusalem. He did not capture the city until the next year, when, after a six months' siege, the city fell, and thus Herod the Great became master of his dominions.

In these days Rome set its own rulers, directly appointed from the imperial city, over some parts of its territory, while over other parts she set native princes under her suzerainty. At the birth of Our Lord, the position of Herod was not unlike that of the Sultan of Egypt, or the Rajah of an Indian state, under the British government at the present day. This explains how it was that, although Herod was king, a decree of Augustus Cæsar, that all the (Roman) world should be "taxed," was effective in Judæa. On the death of Herod the Great in A.D. 2 there were two rival claimants for the throne, Archelaus and Herod Antipas. The case for the rival claimants was considered at Rome. Archelaus became nominal ruler of Jerusalem. On complaints being made as to his methods of government, he was removed, and Roman procurators were appointed instead. The most famous of these procurators was Pontius Pilate. This, then, was the position of affairs at the time of the ministry and death of Our Lord. Thus we understand why Our Lord was brought before the High Priest, and was tried for an offence against the Jewish law, how the consent of the representative of Rome was necessary for the sentence of death, and how it was that the soldiery employed were not Jews, but Roman soldiers of the army of occupation.

The greatest invasion of Palestine by the Romans was that under Titus, when Jerusalem underwent a siege more terrible, and a destruction more complete, than any on record. This is that foretold by Our Lord Himself : " If thou hadst known, even thou, at least in this thy day, the things which belong unto thy peace ! but now they are hid from thine eyes. For the days shall come upon thee, that thine enemies shall cast a trench about thee, and compass thee round, and keep thee in on every side, and shall lay thee even with the ground, and thy children within thee, and they shall not leave in thee one stone upon another ; because thou knowest not the time of thy visitation." [1]

We must trace shortly the events that led up to, and culminated in, this great siege. The campaign was not an original invasion of Judæa but rather a re-conquest or punitive expedition. At all times the Jews proved themselves truculent subjects of the Roman Empire. Fanatically religious or blindly

[1] St. Luke xix. 41–44.

superstitious, they believed that, come what might, Jehovah would fight upon their side and give victory to His chosen people. Had He not destroyed the host of Sennacherib to save His Holy City? Would He not so cause all the enemies of Israel to perish? With overweening arrogance and inconceivable self-confidence, they, a mere handful of men, thus offered battle to the Mistress of the World.

Ever impatient of discipline, and anxious to regain their complete liberty, the Jews fretted at the rule of Rome. Little by little there grew up a state of irritation between the Roman authorities and the Jews, which reached a climax in A.D. 64, when one Florus was appointed Procurator. He ruled with a high hand, and, as was not uncommon with Roman governors, set about enriching himself at the expense of his subjects. By sending his soldiers into the city to kill and plunder he sought to inspire the Jews with proper respect for Rome; he merely exasperated them into revolt.

The insurgents captured the fortress of Antonia from the Romans, and Florus, unable to maintain his position in Jerusalem, left there a small garrison, and retired to Cæsarea. The turbulent element in Jerusalem massacred this garrison; revolts followed in other parts of the country; and Palestine was soon ablaze with insurrection. Cestius, the Governor of Syria, assembling a large army at Antioch, marched southwards to Jerusalem, and laid siege to the city. Just as the city was on the point of surrender, he, for some unknown reason, raised the siege and withdrew. The retreating Romans were pursued by the Jews with darts, with stones and with insults. The retreat became a flight; Cestius and his army sustained the most terrible disgrace that had ever befallen Roman arms in the East. Could anything have happened more calculated to rouse the indignation of the haughty Romans, and at the same time to convince the superstitious Jews of the infallibility of their divine protection?

The Emperor Nero, realizing the seriousness of the situation, despatched Vespasian, one of the ablest Roman generals, with as fine a Roman army as had ever been put into the field. Vespasian landed at Acre, where he assembled a force of some sixty thousand men. Profiting by the experience of Cestius, he made no attempt to move up into the hills against Jerusalem, until he had first reduced the whole of the surrounding country. He marched into Galilee, where he spent a couple of years in subduing the many fortified cities in that province held by the Jews. This task accomplished, and the whole surrounding country having been reduced as far round as Jericho, Vespasian returned to Cæsarea to make preparations for the siege of Jerusalem. But his victorious career in Palestine was crowned by a yet higher honour at home. Returning to Rome he was proclaimed Emperor, while in Palestine his mantle fell upon his son Titus.

What had been happening in Jerusalem itself, during the four years that elapsed between the retreat of Cestius and the advance of Titus? Had the Jews been emulating Hezekiah, and, in view of the imminent storm, been improving the fortifications of the city and preparing to withstand the siege? Had they sunk all petty differences in order that the foe might be met with a united front? Far from it. During all this time the city had been torn asunder by internal dissension. No less than three distinct factions were at first engaged in this mad civil war. They slew one another; they burnt the reserves of grain; they had scarcely patched up their quarrels when the Roman army arrived at the very walls. The Christians appear to have left the city early during the war and migrated East of the Jordan, so that probably few or none of them were present throughout the agonies of the siege. On the other hand the investment of the city coincided with the Feast of the Passover. At this feast it was the custom of the Jews from all outlying quarters of the country to flock into the Holy City. The normal population was therefore swollen out of all proportion to the accommodation. It will thus be appreciated that, on the arrival of the Roman army, the internal condition of the city was already well-nigh hopeless. But the people, and especially their leaders, were fired with implacable hostility to the Romans, stubborn determination to fight on to the bitter end, and blind confidence in the supernatural.

A.D. 70 was the fateful year. Leaving Cæsarea in March, Titus moved up into the hills and then advanced southward against Jerusalem along the great North road. He encountered no opposition upon the way, and on the 11th April reached the city. Part of his army encamped upon the Mount of Olives on the east, and part on the north and north-west.

It was decided to begin the assault with the north-western part of the wall. All the trees around Jerusalem were cut down for the construction of the necessary engines of war. The walls were battered, and in a short space a breach was effected. The outer defences had fallen within a fortnight of the commencement of the siege. A parade of the Roman army was then held beneath the walls in order that Titus, like Joshua of old, might impress the miserable citizens within of the strength of his host, and of the uselessness of their resistance. The Jewish leaders would not hear of surrender.

Titus used his best endeavours to induce the city to capitulate, and sent Josephus the historian, who was in the Roman camp, to speak to the citizens in their own language; for he imagined that they might yield to the persuasion of a countryman of their own. Josephus reasoned with them, appealing to the past history of the nation, pointing out that Pharaoh and the Egyptians, and Sennacherib and the Assyrians had all been overthrown, not by the act of the people, but through the act of God, not by the strength of their arms but in answer to their prayers. He pointed out how often the Jewish nation had failed when it had had recourse to arms. He impressed upon them the necessity of pure and sinless lives if they expected their prayers to be heard and answered. " As for you," he said, " what have you done of those things that are recommended by our legislator! and what have you not done of those things that he hath condemned! How much more impious are you than those who were so quickly taken! You are quarrelling about rapines and murders, and invent strange ways of wickedness. And, after all this, do you expect him whom you have so impiously abused to be your supporter?" But the defenders were obdurate. Nothing would dissuade them from carrying on resistance to the bitter end.

The miseries within the city were indescribable. Some of the wretched citizens tried to desert, and at first a great number of them were allowed to escape into the country, whither they pleased. However, John and Simon, the leaders of the factions within, "did more carefully watch these men's going out than they did the coming in of the Romans; and, if any one did but afford the least shadow of suspicion of such an intention, his throat was cut immediately."

Josephus' graphic description of the agonies that these poor wretches suffered forms a chapter of horrors, from which we must quote, but a couple of extracts will suffice :—

"The famine was too hard for all other passions, and it is destructive to nothing so much as to modesty. For what was otherwise worthy of reverence was in this case despised; insomuch that children pulled the very morsels that their fathers were eating out of their very mouths, and, what was still more to be pitied, so did the mothers do as to their infants. And when those that were most dear were perishing under their hands, they were not ashamed to take from them the very last drops that might preserve their lives. And while they ate after this manner, yet were they not concealed in so doing. But the seditious everywhere came upon them immediately, and snatched away from them what they had gotten from others. For when they saw any house shut up, this was to them a signal that the people within had gotten some food. Whereupon they broke open the doors and ran in, and took pieces of what they were eating almost out of their very throats and this by force. The old men who held their food fast, were beaten; and if the women hid what they had within their hands, their hair was torn for so doing. Nor was there any commiseration shown either to the aged or to infants, but they lifted up children from the ground as they hung upon the morsels they had gotten, and shook them down upon the floor. But still were they more barbarously cruel to those that had prevented their coming in, and had actually swallowed down what they were going to seize upon, as if they had been unjustly defrauded of their right. They also invented terrible methods of torments to discover where any food was. And a man was forced to bear what it is terrible even to hear, in order to make him confess that he had but one loaf of bread, or that he might discover a handful of barley meal that was concealed. And this was done when the tormentors were not themselves hungry. For the thing had been less barbarous had necessity forced them to it. But this was done to keep their madness in exercise, and as making preparation of provisions for themselves for the following days. These men went also to meet those that had crept out of the city by night, as far as the Roman guards, to gather some plants and herbs that grew wild. And when these people thought they had got clear of the enemy, they snatched from them what they had brought with them, and they were to be well contented that they were only spoiled, and not slain at the same time."

Josephus goes on to describe the terrible fate of those who tried to desert, or merely stole out to forage for roots, and fell into the hands of the Romans. For the leniency at first shown by Titus towards deserters, did not long continue.

"Titus then sent a party of horsemen, and ordered they should lay ambushes for those that went out into the valleys to gather food. The greater part of them were poor people, who were deterred from deserting by the concern they were under for their own relations. For they could not hope to escape away, together with their wives and children, without the knowledge of the seditious. Nor could they think of leaving these relations to be slain by the robbers on their account. Nay, the severity of the famine made them bold in thus going out. So nothing remained but that, when they were concealed from the robbers, they should be taken by the enemy. They were first whipped, and then tormented with all sorts of tortures before they died, and were then crucified before the wall of the city. They caught every day some five hundred Jews; nay, some days they caught more. The Roman soldiers, out of the wrath and hatred they bore the Jews, nailed those they caught, one after one way, and another after another, to the crosses, by way of jest; when their multitude was so great, that room was wanting for the crosses, and crosses wanting for the bodies."

Within the city the famine spread its clutches and devoured the people by whole houses and families. The upper rooms were full of women and children that were dying by famine, and the lanes of the city were full of the dead bodies of the aged.

At first orders were given that the dead should be buried out of the public treasury, as the stench of their bodies could not be endured. But afterwards, when this could no longer be done, they were cast down from the walls into the valleys beneath, which valleys soon became thick with putrefying corpses.

Some deserters did succeed in gaining admission to the Roman camp. But their lot was no more fortunate. To provide for their future welfare they swallowed pieces of gold before leaving the city, subsequently recovering them in a manner not necessary to describe. Learning that these deserters were full of money, many of the undisciplined followers of the Roman army cut open these wretched creatures to see whether their bodies contained gold. Of a truth Josephus had a taste for the depiction of horrors. But then he himself writes, with becoming modesty, of his mother having had " the advantage of bringing so extraordinary a person as this son into the world " !

The reduction of the city was steadily pressed forward. Battering rams and catapults, mines and countermines were all made use of. The fortress of Antonia was taken, and the Jews were driven back into the Temple. Still the Jews fought with the fierceness of tigers. Little by little the Romans fought their way onward through the outer courts until on the 12th August the Temple was captured and burnt. Titus himself was anxious to save the glorious temple of Herod, which he considered would be an ornament to the Roman government of Jerusalem. But one of the Roman soldiers " without staying for any orders, and without any concern or dread upon him at so great an undertaking, and being hurried only by a certain divine fury, snatched somewhat out of the materials that were on fire, and being lifted up by another soldier he set fire to " a portion of the Temple, which soon was wrapt in flames. Both the Jews and the Roman soldiers strove to stay the fire—but in vain. The Temple was destroyed for ever, after a period, according to Josephus, of eleven hundred and thirty years since its original foundation by Solomon.

Even yet Jerusalem was not completely reduced. The upper city indeed still held out; but the heart of the Jews had gone. A breach was made in the remaining defences, whereupon the Jews, abandoning further effort, endeavoured to escape. The Romans, pouring into the town, began by slaying indiscriminately. They stood aghast at the appalling sights which met their eyes; entire families of dead that had died of the famine. Yet they carried on with the massacre of those that remained alive, so that the very lanes were obstructed with the dead bodies, while the whole city ran with blood to such a degree that the fire of many of the houses was quenched with the blood of the victims. The city of Jerusalem was, as Our Lord had prophesied, completely demolished, not one stone was left upon another.

Titus returned by way of Cæsarea to Rome, where the vanquished leaders Simon and John graced his triumph. The Jewish nation as a nation had ceased to exist. Palestine had become wholly and absolutely Roman.

Yet one more attempt was made to throw off the yoke of Rome and to re-establish the Jews as a nation. After the total destruction of Jerusalem by Titus, it became merely a fortified Roman Camp. In A.D. 130 the Jews rose again under one Barcochebas. At first the Jews met with some success, and captured the Roman camp at Jerusalem. But they were overwhelmed by the Romans, who with a firm relentless hand soon put down this, the last and the wildest of all the Jewish revolts. The Emperor Hadrian resolved to suppress this troublesome and turbulent Judaism altogether. He turned Jerusalem into a Roman colony, calling it Aelia Capitolina, forbade any Jew on pain of death to appear even within sight of the city, and on the site of the Temple he built a Temple to Jupiter.

Palestine pursued the even tenor of its uneventful way for

the next couple of centuries. It was only when the Emperor Constantine embraced Christianity, and adopted it as the religion of the Roman empire, that Palestine again came into prominence, this time as a Christian country. Monasteries, churches, and religious houses sprung up throughout the land. Pilgrims flocked to the Holy Sepulchre. Jerusalem became the religious focus of the West.

When, in A.D. 395, the partition of the Roman empire was effected, Palestine became part of the Eastern or Byzantine empire. Thenceforth it owed allegiance no longer to Rome, but to Constantinople. Peace and prosperity continued so long as the Byzantine empire continued strong enough to keep invaders at a distance. As that empire grew effete, so war again began to trouble Palestine. Within about twenty years the country was invaded by two distinct Asiatic peoples, the Persians and the Arabs. The former was the more destructive and transient occupation; the latter the more benign and permanent.

Not once nor twice in the age-long history of Palestine has this unfortunate country been swept by incursions of wild hordes from Central Asia, short, sharp, but terribly destructive. Cambyses, Chosroes, the Kharezmians, are but three examples, widely divergent in period. It was one of these incursions which now shook the Byzantine Empire to its foundations. In A.D. 614 Chosroes the Persian, who had already overrun Syria and Asia Minor, sent an army into Palestine to capture this country from the Byzantines. Thousands of discontented Jews, thirsting for vengeance against the Christians, flocked to his standard. Jerusalem was badly prepared for defence and fell to the Persians after little or no resistance. A terrible massacre of the inhabitants followed, not less than sixty and possibly nearer ninety thousand being slain. Destroying as it went, the Persian army swept onward into Egypt. Their career of success lasted for little more than a decade. The Byzantine Emperor, Heraclius, freeing Constantinople from the attack of the Persians, drove them back into Armenia; and then, pursuing his victories, he advanced into Persia, where Chosroes was utterly defeated and taken prisoner. Heraclius returned in triumph to Jerusalem.

It appeared that the Asiatic peril had passed. Thanksgivings were offered up at the Holy City, and a commencement was made with the rebuilding of the Christian churches which the Persians had destroyed. It seemed as though Christianity in Palestine might look forward to a long and uninterrupted period of prosperity. But it was not to be. In less than ten years after Heraclius' triumphant return to Jerusalem, the whole country had gone down before the rising tide of Islam.

CHAPTER VIII

THE ARABS

THE Mohammedan era dates from the year A.D. 622. This was the date when the exiled Mahomet fled from Mecca to Medina, and may be regarded as about the time when his teaching and inspiration definitely assumed the form of a religion. In early days his religious views were not antagonistic either to Judaism or to Christianity. The hostility was a later development. Owing to this subsequent hostility, which much increased when the Moslems possessed themselves of the Holy Places of Christendom, and which reached its climax in the Crusades, the close relationship which really exists between those three religions is apt to be overlooked. Mohammedanism, like Christianity, is based upon Judaism. It is, in fact, based upon Judaism plus Christianity. In many respects, such as, for example, polygamy, circumcision and the prohibition of carved images, the laws of Islam adhere more closely to the Mosaic laws than do those of Christendom. All the prophets whom the Christian venerates, including Christ Himself, are venerated by the Moslem, with the addition of the (to them) greatest of prophets Mahomet. Thus it will be understood that the sacred sites of the Holy Land are as sacred to the Moslem as they are to the Christian and the Jew.

The latter part of Mahomet's life was much absorbed with wars in Arabia. Further expeditions were in contemplation, when, in A.D. 632, the Prophet passed away. He was suc-

THE ARABS

ceeded by Abu Bakr, the First Caliph, who carried through the contemplated expeditions. Within a year of the Prophet's death, the sway of Islam had thus been established throughout the Arabian peninsula. But this did not suffice the restless Arabs. Fired with zeal for their new religion they looked further afield. The fertile land of Syria, invitingly near, was naturally among the first of foreign countries to attract their attention.

The campaign in Syria opened in the year following the Prophet's death. An attempt was first made to rally the friendly tribes on the Syrian frontier, whereupon the Byzantine garrisons summoned their Bedouin allies, and assumed a threatening attitude. The first Arab leader in this field, having routed a Syrian column near the Dead Sea, was decoyed by the Byzantine general towards Damascus. He had reached as far as the east of the Sea of Tiberias, when the Byzantines closed in upon his rear, cutting off his retreat. The leader himself fled; but his force was rallied by others, and took up a strong position on the frontier, until further help should arrive from Medina.

Meanwhile Arabia had been entirely pacified, and Abu Bakr was thus able, as the columns returned from the South, to send them off to Syria, to retrieve the fortunes of Islam in that country. Four columns were formed, including sheikhs of renown, with at least a thousand Companions, men who had seen and conversed with the Prophet, all holding themselves at the absolute disposal of the Commander of the Faithful.

These four columns, gathering on the Syrian border, were at first strung out somewhat in echelon in positions overawing the chief Palestine cities. Acting on the advice of Abu Bakr, however, the columns were concentrated on a spot south of the Yarmuk River, near the point where it is crossed by the high road from Damascus. The Yarmuk, which falls into the Jordan a little to the south of the Lake of Galilee, takes its rise in the high lands of the Hauran, and runs in a deep and rugged gorge far beneath the level of the surrounding country. By forming a loop about the point in question, the river leaves on its northern bank a wide plain, the field of Wacusa, bounded on three sides by a sheer precipice and almost closed in on the fourth by a ravine. The Byzantine army spread themselves out upon this plain, and the Arabs, crossing to the north, took up a position commanding the exit. Two months passed away in indecisive skirmishing. Abu Bakr, anxious at the delay and the lack of fire with which the operations were being conducted, summoned Khalid from Lower Mesopotamia, and ordered him to move with reinforcements to the Yarmuk and to take over the direction of operations in that theatre.

The Syrian Desert lay between Khalid and his new sphere of action. He could not follow the northerly and normal route from the Euphrates Valley because of hostile tribes and Byzantine garrisons. So he had no alternative but to cross the Desert as far as Duma, which lay midway between the head of the Red Sea and of the Persian Gulf. From here he took the direct road north-west towards Syria, and would, in a few days, have reached Bostra. But, fearing lest the enemy opposing him in that direction should hinder his junction with the Moslem army on the Yarmuk, he formed the bold design of striking north, right across the waterless and pathless desert, emerging at Tadmor, and thus turning the flank of the Byzantine army. His method of solving the water problem on this march is interesting, though it seems to us wasteful. He gave instructions for as many camels as possible to be gathered, first withheld from water for a while, then allowed to drink plentifully twice, and then to have their ears bound and their lips slit so that they should not ruminate and the water be lost. At each stage across the wilderness ten such camels were slain for each troop of a hundred lances. The water drawn from their bodies was mixed with milk for the horses, while the men were given but a single draught each day. On the fifth day the supply gave out, and, although by this time they should have reached a neighbourhood where there was water, yet none was to be found. Khalid gave orders for a search to be made for a bramble bush. At last they came across a half-concealed root; here they dug down into the ground, and their search was rewarded by the discovery of a plentiful supply of water.

They were now on the Syrian side of the Desert about a hundred miles east of Damascus. The neighbourhood was surprised, Tadmor was attacked, and, after a slight resistance, yielded. Then, turning south or south-west, Khalid skirted the Hauran within sight of Damascus, and eventually effected a junction with the Moslem army which still lay inactive on the Yarmuk.

The Byzantine army must have largely outnumbered the Moslem; but it was disunited, divided by the schisms of Christianity, and with its Bedouin personnel more in sympathy with the Desert Arabs than with the Byzantine Christians. The Arab army, on the other hand, of which Khalid now assumed the supreme command, was bound together as one man, fired with zeal to fight in the ways of the Lord, and with the promise of loot upon Earth and of salvation in Heaven.

The decisive battle of Wacusa on the Yarmuk was fought towards the end of August A.D. 634, little more than a couple of years after the death of the Prophet. The Byzantine army advanced, but they were much handicapped by the desertion, at the commencement of the battle, of a number of Bedouins who went over to the Arabs. Nevertheless the battle raged all day, and the carnage on both sides was great. Towards evening the Byzantines began to falter. The cavalry, with nothing behind them but the precipice, charged upon the Arabs, who opened to let them pass through. Gaining the open country they galloped away, never to reappear. The Arabs then drove down upon the remaining force, hemmed in by the surrounding chasm; those who escaped the sword were hurled in living mass into the yawning gulf. The next morning found the Arabs in silent possession of the plain. The fate of the Byzantine army struck terror into the Byzantine Court and people. Though more fighting still lay ahead, yet the opposition that remained was but poor and feeble; the fate of Syria was sealed.

Meanwhile Abu Bakr had died, and had been succeeded in the Caliphate by Omar. The first act of the latter was to remove Khalid from the supreme command of the army in Syria and order him to hand over the command to Abu Obeida. The messenger arrived just as the Byzantine army was advancing for the battle of Wacusa. Khalid kept the message to himself until after the battle had been fought and won, and then loyally handed over to Abu Obeida. But Obeida, knowing the military genius of Khalid, was wise and magnanimous enough to act largely upon his advice, and thus Khalid remained virtually the chief captain of Islam in the West.

From Wacusa the invading army marched northwards. News reached it that Damascus had been reinforced, and that in the Arab rear the scattered fragments of the defeated Byzantine army had re-formed in the Valley of the Jordan. A strong column was accordingly sent back to hold in check the enemy on the Jordan, while the main army advanced upon Damascus. This city was invested, but every attempt to breach the massive walls failed. Months passed by, yet the Arabs did not withdraw, nor did Heraclius, the Byzantine emperor who was then at Hims (Emessa), succeed in creating a diversion. The hopes of the invested Damascenes dwindled to despair.

One day the Governor of the city made a feast to the garrison. The Arabs decided to take advantage of this night to capture the city. The Arab army was at this time divided tactically, with Khalid and a part of the force on one side of the city, and Obeida with the remainder on the other. Khalid's force succeeded in crossing the moat and scaling the wall. The defending garrison at this point was overwhelmed. The gate from within was forced open, and Khalid's column poured in, slaying and sacking all around. On the other side of the city the Governor had meanwhile tendered his submission to Obeida, and so, to the disgust of Khalid's column, the sack and carnage were stayed. Damascus became, and for nearly thirteen centuries remained, a Moslem city.

In the meantime the Byzantine force further south had been kept inactive in the neighbourhood of Beisan, where the Plains of Esdraelon and the Vale of Jezreel meet the Valley of the Jordan. Here a force had collected eighty thousand strong. To secure their front they dammed the streams and turned the vale into a marsh. In this way they not only shut the enemy out, but they also shut themselves in. The force, which the Arabs had detached for the purpose, took up a position on the other side of the Jordan Valley at Fihl, and watched. After the fall of Damascus, the main body of the Arabs, fresh from their capture of that city, were anxious to continue their march northwards and to attack Heraclius himself at Hims. But Omar forbade advance so long as an army was in the rear. Accordingly Obeida and Khalid marched south, crossed the Yarmuk, and, moving down the Valley of the Jordan, encamped under Fihl. Here they relieved the force which had been watching the Byzantines, and which force then moved round towards Tiberias to check any attempt of the enemy to get away in that direction. The Byzantine army, hoping to fall upon the Arabs and take them by surprise, suddenly appeared upon the Arabs' flank. Here they met with a warm reception, and there ensued a battle as fierce and obstinate as any that had yet taken place. The Byzantines were again completely defeated, the greater part were caught in the marsh, and few escaped the sword. Another battle, bloody and decisive, was thus added to the many fought out at the Plain of Esraelon.

The Arabs pursued their victorious course northwards. They repulsed a Byzantine attempt to recapture Damascus, stormed Baalbek, and marched upon Hims, which they invested. When the siege had been protracted many weeks, an earthquake breached the battlements. The Governor, finding the position no longer tenable, capitulated. Town after town fell before the victorious advance of the Arabs until Aleppo and Antioch were in their hands. The Byzantine emperor Heraclius retired to Constantinople; and the Moslem Arabs were left masters of Syria.

Throughout these operations the Arab advanced base had been at Jabia, a town on the high land to the east of the sea of Galilee. This place was in communication with the Hejaz and Medina by the pilgrim route east of the Dead Sea. From Jabia the Arab columns could operate northwards against Damascus, or westwards against Tiberias, the Jordan and Southern Palestine. In Southern Palestine, with Egypt in its rear and Cæsarea open to the sea, the Byzantine power was still unbroken. Gaza, Ramleh and Jerusalem were heavily garrisoned. Advancing through Beisan, the Arab army met the Byzantine and defeated it to the west of Jerusalem. The way now lay open to the Holy City. Before going up thither, however, the Arab leader, Amru, took the precaution to secure his rear by capturing Gaza, Ludd, Joppa and other places, until at length the only cities remaining in the hands of the Christians were Ramleh and Jerusalem.

The Byzantine leader now retired with his army to Egypt. The Patriarch of Jerusalem sued for peace. He stipulated as a condition of his surrender that Omar should himself come to the Holy City, and there in person settle the capitulation. The Caliph Omar consented and came up from Medina. Terms were agreed upon, terms which, though severe, are generally regarded as showing Omar's magnanimity. To the Christians were guaranteed safety both of person and property, without interference on the part of the Moslems with any of their religious exercises, houses, or institutions.

Omar then made a tour of the Holy City. His stay was but

THE ARABS

a short one and he returned to Medina. At the temple area he erected a mosque, a simple square building of timber. The glorious "Mosque of Omar," commemorating his name, which stands upon the temple area, and is the pride of Jerusalem to this day, was not erected until some sixty years later.

Thus all Syria had become Moslem, and, except for the short period of the Crusading kingdom of Jerusalem, it so continued down to the British conquest of 1918; a period of nearly thirteen centuries.

How strangely the history of the Holy Land repeats itself! Twenty centuries previously a people, desert born and bred, trained to war in campaigns against desert tribes, just emerging as a race of conquerors, and fired with religious zeal for the one and only God, had swept up by the caravan route from the south-east, had invaded Palestine, carrying all before them, and had planted therein the intensely monotheistic and iconoclastic religion of Judaism. Now the Arabs, under conditions and by routes so similar, had invaded Palestine, carrying all before them, and had planted therein the equally monotheistic and iconoclastic religion of Islam.

Yet another parallelism. Thirteen centuries ago the forces of the ruler of the Hejaz moved up by the route east of the Dead Sea and the Jordan and captured Damascus, wresting it from the ancient Byzantine empire, which, established at Constantinople, had for centuries dominated Asia Minor and Syria, but had then reached a condition of decadence. To-day it has been reserved to us to witness the forces of another ruler of the Hejaz move up by the route east of the Dead Sea and the Jordan to the capture of Damascus from another Empire, likewise established at Constantinople, which has for centuries dominated Asia Minor and Syria, and is now, like its predecessor, tottering in decay.

IX

THE CRUSADES

AFTER the conquest of Jerusalem by the Arabs, the Christians were allowed a reasonable measure of religious freedom. Although the city changed hands from time to time, yet on the whole the Christians were allowed to use their places of worship, and pilgrims were unmolested, for a period of close upon four-and-a-half centuries.

In A.D. 1077 Jerusalem was wrested from the Arabs by the Seljuk Turks, who, though nominally Moslem, were a semi-barbarous people from Central Asia. Thereupon commenced a period of persecution. The hapless pilgrims were robbed on the road, and then refused admission to the Holy City on account of their poverty. Many of them died, without even reaching the city. Even if they got within the walls they were not much safer, for there they were insulted, mocked, spat upon, and beaten, while fanatical crowds outraged their most sacred ceremonies.

Among the crowd of pilgrims that visited the Holy City about this time was one Peter the Hermit. His indignation knew no bounds. Armed with letters from the Patriarch of Jerusalem addressed to the sovereign powers of Europe, he started forth to preach the crusade. The Pope received him with ardour and authorized him to preach over the whole of Europe. In town and village, in pulpit and by the roadside, the eloquence of his words proved irresistible. He gathered to his standard the virtuous, zealous for Christ, the sinners,

THE CRUSADES

anxious to expiate their sins, old and young, men and women, rich and poor, all eager to share the burden of the Cross.

At this time the remnant of the Christian or Byzantine Empire of the East was in peril of the Turks, even at its very capital, Constantinople. The Turks had conquered the whole of Asia Minor, which they were then holding by garrisons. The Emperor of the East, Alexis, had implored help from the West to check this menace. The Pope thought he saw, in the Crusades, an opportunity of placing the Eastern Church under an obligation to the Western, and so in a state of subservience to Rome. Thus, with the official assistance of no crowned head, but with the benediction of all, the Christians of the West embarked upon the campaign, with the twofold object of helping the Christians of the East, and of recovering the Holy Sepulchre.

In the spring of 1096, the first portion of the army of the Crusaders gathered on the banks of the Meuse. They numbered a hundred thousand men bearing arms, besides a mixed multitude of old men, women and children. Peter the Hermit was elected leader. The host started on its march across Europe to Constantinople in two bodies. Marching down the Rhine, little difficulty was experienced by the first column, while passing through Germany and Hungary, where the Crusaders were regarded with benevolent neutrality. But on entering Bulgaria their troubles commenced in earnest. Permission to buy provisions having been refused, they left their camp and dispersed about the country foraging. In revenge, a large number of these marauders were killed by the Bulgars. The second column commenced its troubles even earlier. They massacred Hungarians on their way through Hungary, while their passage through Bulgaria was yet more unfortunate.

At length the two columns united at Constantinople. Although wholly lacking in military genius, organization, and discipline, and against the advice of the Emperor Alexis, the host at once crossed into Asia Minor under the lead of Peter the Hermit. In spite of losses by the way, their gaps doubtless filled by fresh adherents, the host seems to have still numbered a hundred thousand fighting men. They attacked Nicœa. But the Sultan of Nicœa ambuscaded the force, and counter-attacked them in front and in rear; thus caught, cooped together in confusion, and badly armed, the Crusaders offered but slight resistance. Of the hundred thousand who had crossed into Asia, but three thousand escaped. The bones of their comrades long stood as a monument to the disaster, whitening 'neath the Eastern sun, and pointing skeleton fingers on the road to Jerusalem.

But now armies of a different calibre assembled in the West; they were composed of stiffer fighting material, better armed, comparatively well disciplined, and commanded by feudal dukes and counts. These armies, starting from different points in Western Europe, and marching by different routes, likewise converged on Constantinople. The numbers which came from Western Europe cannot be approximately stated, but, counting men, women, children and camp-followers, probably reached a million. The fighting men are said to have comprised a hundred thousand knights and half a million foot-soldiers; but this is probably an exaggeration.

Several months had elapsed since the destruction of Peter the Hermit's force, when this more formidable army of Crusaders crossed from Europe into Asia Minor. The miserable refugees from Peter's Army, who had been living hidden in the forest, now emerged, and, showing the plain where their companions' bones lay whitening in the sun, told the tale of their misfortunes. The indignant Crusaders demanded to be instantly led against Nicœa. To avenge that massacre the city was besieged, and captured; then the Crusaders resumed their onward march towards the Holy Land.

Their next collision with the Turks was at a place called the Valley of Gorgona. Here, after a hardly-contested battle, the Crusaders defeated the Saracens, who fled in utter disorder, leaving a large number of dead on the field, and abandoning their camp and baggage. While the Crusaders were enjoying the booty that had thus fallen into their hands, the enemy were retreating southwards, devastating and destroying as they went.

The Crusaders then set out upon a terrible march across Asia Minor. The supply arrangements were bad; their attempt to live on the country was largely frustrated by the action of the retreating Turks. Their path lay through Phrygia, a wild, sterile and waterless country. The road was strewn with the bodies of those who died of sunstroke or thirst; no less than five hundred died on the march of but a single day.

Thus they reached Antiocheia, the former capital of Pisidia. From here advance parties were sent forward which captured Tarsus and Adana, important towns near the extreme northeast corner of the Mediterranean. At Tarsus violent quarrels unfortunately arose among the Crusaders. Tancred's force attacked that of Baldwin. A battle followed; but the night brought reflection, and next morning, reconciliation.

Meanwhile the Crusading army pressed on. They crossed the Taurus Mountains and sat down to besiege Antioch, the modern Antakia, near the sea, some fifty miles or so due west of Aleppo. The siege dragged on, the privations of the besiegers, amongst whom food was terribly short, being worse than those of the besieged. Eventually the town was taken in June, 1098, through the treachery of one of the defenders. The Crusaders entered into possession and enjoyment of the city. But their enjoyment was short-lived. A larger Moslem host came up, and the Crusaders were themselves besieged. After more privations, and when the position seemed desperate, a miracle was alleged to have been performed; the spearhead which pierced the body of Our Lord was miraculously discovered. Fired with enthusiasm by this revelation of God's active sympathy with their cause, the Crusaders moved out and encountered the Moslems, fighting as only religious enthusiasts can fight. The Moslems were routed with enormous slaughter, their rich and luxurious camp falling into the hands of the conquerors. Plenty followed famine; but pestilence soon followed plenty. Eager though they were to push on to Jerusalem, they had perforce to remain at Antioch until the heat of summer had passed, and health had come again with the winter breezes.

In November the onward march to Jerusalem was resumed. The army marched in two divisions, part following the valley of the Orontes, and part the road by the sea. The two divisions met at Tripoli, and then the whole force took the coast road by Beirut, Tyre, and Haifa to Jaffa and Ramleh. Having gained such a decisive victory at Antioch, they were not much molested in the course of their southward march. Though the coast towns were held by the enemy, the Crusaders left them untouched, and the townsmen, on the other hand, did not oppose the march of the Crusaders.

Meanwhile the Fatemite Khalif of Cairo had driven out the Turks and had placed Egyptian garrisons in Jerusalem and the other towns of Palestine. The primary object of the Crusades, the expulsion of the Turks from Palestine, had therefore already been achieved. But the intention of the Crusaders was, not merely to expel the Turks, but to drive out the Moslems of whatever nationality, and to take Jerusalem for themselves. Accordingly the embassies sent by the Fatemite Khalif, to welcome the Crusaders and to inform them that the privileges of the Christians would be restored, were coldly received. They were told that the only way to avoid attack was to surrender the city at once; and this the Egyptian governor naturally refused to do.

At Ramleh the Crusading host was met by a party of Christians from Bethlehem with prayers to them to protect their town. Tancred with a hundred knights rode off to Bethlehem and Jerusalem, where they made a reconnaissance. And then the Crusading host, moving probably by the Valley of Ajalon, came up from Ramleh and laid siege to Jerusalem. The army which sat down to the siege numbered about forty thousand, all told, the miserable remnant of the army of six hundred thousand fighting men or more with which Godfrey had taken Nicœa. Out of the million or so who had set out upon the Crusade, barely four per cent. had reached the Holy City.

The garrison of Jerusalem had not been idle. A store of provisions had been laid up within the city in anticipation of a siege. The fortifications generally had been improved and the garrison strengthened. Immediately before the arrival of the Crusaders, the Christians within the walls were expelled.

The Crusaders pitched their camp on the north side of the city, no attack on the other sides being possible owing to the deep valleys with which the city was, and is, protected. At first the Crusaders were so fanatical that, disdaining the aid of engines of war, they rushed forward, protected only by their bucklers, and tried to breach the walls with pikes and hammers. Boiling oil and pitch soon taught these ardent spirits a lesson. Such methods were quickly abandoned in favour of others more in accordance with the stage then reached by military science. The construction of wooden towers was put in hand. Much difficulty was experienced owing to the lack of suitable timber, until the situation was opportunely saved by the arrival of a Genoese fleet at Joppa with stores, provisions, and timber, together with a large number of Genoese artificers and carpenters.

The sufferings which the Crusaders now endured from lack of water were as bad as any they had experienced in their march across Asia Minor. The nearest available wells were six or seven miles away. Parties were sent out to scour for water, many of whom, while thus wandering in search of wells, were cut off and killed by the enemy. It must be remembered that no rain falls upon the Judæan hills throughout the summer and that the so-called brooks about Jerusalem, such as the brook Kedron, are only dry water courses carrying off the surface water during the winter rains. (The city itself is supplied with water stored in capacious cisterns and supplemented from a spring.) Their sufferings from lack of water in the heat of a Syrian summer were intense; they sucked the earth, they licked the dew, they drank the blood of beasts. Their sufferings, their necessities, their religious enthusiasm, all demanded that the city should be assaulted immediately; a protracted siege was out of the question.

With the aid of the timber brought by the Genoese ships, three great towers were constructed, high enough to overlook the walls, each with a sort of drawbridge on the top, which could be lowered so as to afford a passage to the wall of the city. On the day preceding that fixed for the assault, a processional march was made round the city, like those of Joshua at Jericho and of Titus at Jerusalem. On the morning of the 14th July 1099 the towers were moved against the walls and the battering was commenced. The fierce fighting on this day was not successful; but on the day following the battle was renewed, the wall was broken in several places, and the efforts of the besieged to set the towers on fire met with failure. The critical moment for the assault had now arrived. St. George is said to have appeared in shining armour. The tower of Godfrey was pushed against the wall; Godfrey leapt across; even the women and children joined in the attack; the Saracens gave way, and Jerusalem was taken.

Then followed a scene of indescribable slaughter. At first all that could be found within the city were put to death. The Crusaders ran through the streets, slaying as they went. We turn from the description of the scene with a sickening feeling of disgust. It may well be that, after their awful privations, and the terrible mortality among their ranks, the feelings of the Crusaders had become blunted, and their respect for human life terribly cheap. But it cannot be forgotten

THE CRUSADES

that theirs was a crusade to right the wrong, and that their aim was to establish upon earth the kingdom of the Prince of Peace.

The First Crusade having now attained its goal, most of the leaders returned to Europe. A Christian kingdom was founded at Jerusalem, of which Godfrey became the first king. He set to work consolidating the kingdom, but only lived for a year, and was succeeded by Baldwin. This king, who was constantly engaged in war with the Egyptians, succeeded in capturing most of the coast towns, with the exception of Tyre and Ascalon. Ascalon was not captured until many years later, while some parts of Syria never fell into the hands of the Crusaders at all.

We cannot attempt a detailed account of the troubled history of this Christian kingdom of Jerusalem. It only lasted for eighty-eight years. Throughout that time it existed as an exotic, and never rested on a sure and stable foundation. It lacked the moral and material support of a great power. It was the child of all Western Europe and therefore protected by none. It was dependent both for its revenue and its recruits upon the stream of Western pilgrims which annually visited the Holy Places. Its people intermarried with the native Syrians and acquired Eastern vices. It was feudal, and laboured therefore under the disadvantages of the feudal system, jealous barons struggling for their own interests and sacrificing those of the state. As we look back upon the history of this little kingdom we wonder, not that its life was so short, but that it lasted at all.

Interesting to the soldier are the two great military religious orders to which this kingdom gave birth. The first was the Order of the Templars. At this time the road between Joppa and Jerusalem was infested with robbers, who preyed upon the pilgrims coming up to the Holy City. It was for the purpose of protecting these pilgrims that the Order of the Templars was instituted. The distinguishing dress of this

Order was a white mantle embroidered with a red cross. To the knights of this order was allotted as a Church the Mosque of Omar on the Temple area, then called the " Temple of the Lord," from which the Order derived its name. The Order was very popular, rapidly increasing in numbers and importance, until it became one of the most powerful bodies in Palestine.

The second great military religious order was that of the Hospital of St. John, otherwise known as the Knights Hospitallers. The object of this Order was the provision of accommodation for the sick and for the reception of Christian pilgrims that came to visit the Holy Places. Their distinguishing dress was a black mantle embroidered with the well-known white eight-pointed cross of the order. These orders, at first a source of strength, subsequently developed into one of weakness. Each became an imperium in imperio, and the poor little Christian kingdom, weak enough at its best, was thus further weakened by the jealousies and contentions of the rival knights.

Fifty years after the First Crusade, this kingdom was already finding itself in sore straits. Wars with the Saracens had been regular occurrences ever since its foundation. For neither the Crusaders nor the Saracens were strong enough to expel the other from Palestine. We have seen that for recruits for its armies, reliance was placed entirely upon Western Europe. An urgent appeal was now made for a grand rally to come to the support of the tottering kingdom. The Second Crusade was preached by Bernard, and the host consisted entirely of French and Germans. The First Crusaders had set off with light and buoyant hearts; the Second set off with gloomy forebodings of misery and suffering, only too well justified. The Second Crusade, like the First, proceeded overland by way of Constantinople. It was in the early winter of 1147 that the Germans, first to reach Constantinople, crossed into Asia Minor. We are told that they reckoned on the friendship of the Greeks, but were grievously disappointed, for the Greeks charged them extravagant prices for the most inferior articles. The army consisted of seventy thousand horse, and a vast multitude of foot-soldiers, women and children. Their guides deserted them. They were caught by the Saracens, and, out of all that host, but seven thousand escaped ; all the rest were slaughtered.

Meanwhile the French, who had been following behind the Germans, had reached Nicœa. From here they decided to take the coast route, and fought their way to Ephesus. They were overtaken by plague so that out of the vast numbers that set out from France and Germany, but a small proportion succeeded in reaching Syria. The army delayed for some time at Antioch, where Raymond, the Christian governor of that city, vainly attempted to divert the crusade to his own purposes. Eventually the army continued its southward journey to Palestine. In June, 1148, a council was held at Acre to decide how the army could best be utilised. It was decided to attempt with it the capture of Damascus, which city had never yet been taken by the Crusaders. Accordingly the army, which, if wisely used, might have helped to buttress the declining fortunes of Jerusalem, was diverted instead to a new and useless expedition. The attempt to capture Damascus was made, but proved an utter failure. The Christians were left with no alternative but retreat ; they broke up their camp and fled ; and that was the end of the Second Crusade. Towards assisting the kingdom of Jerusalem, it had effected absolutely nothing. On the other hand, by forestalling the supply of pilgrims, and thus anticipating the normal flow of recruits that would otherwise have become available for the army of Jerusalem, the Second Crusade did more harm than good to that unhappy kingdom.

The Crusading kingdom of Jerusalem dragged out a precarious existence for yet another forty years, when it fell at length before the armies of Saladin, whose rise we must now briefly consider. Save for its seaboard this Christian kingdom was surrounded on all sides by Moslem territory. On the north, the Seljuk Sultan of Damascus acknowledged the supremacy of the Abbaside Khalif. On the south, Egypt was under the rival Fatemite Khalif of Cairo. These two rivals were independent and generally hostile. The kingdom of Jerusalem thus owed its continued independence in no small degree to the rivalries of Damascus and Cairo.

In A.D. 1167 the Seljuk Sultan of Damascus invaded and conquered Egypt, bringing Cairo under the power of Damascus. Saladin was made Grand Vizier of Egypt. He soon made himself master of the country, did away with the Fatemite dynasty, and proclaimed the Abbaside Khalif as the head of Islam. The position of Jerusalem was thereby completely changed. It now lay surrounded by territory owning allegiance to but one ruler, the Seljuk Sultan of Damascus. War followed. The Sultan, Nur ed Din, advanced from the north into Moab, east of the Jordan, while Saladin invaded from the south. On this occasion they were defeated, and Moab was recaptured by the Christians. In 1174 Nur ed Din died; and Saladin, having made himself Sultan of Damascus, became the most powerful ruler in the East.

It was in 1182 that Saladin, having firmly established himself in his usurped sultanate of Damascus, turned his attention to the conquest of the Christian kingdom of Jerusalem. Pitching at Tiberias, he harassed the neighbourhood of Beisan, Jabin, and the Jordan Valley, causing much loss of life and property to the Christians. Year after year he engaged in such operations, which, though generally successful, partook rather of the character of border forays than of regular warfare.

The year 1187 sealed the doom of the Christian Kingdom. Saladin, assembling a great army at Damascus, crossed the Jordan south of the Sea of Galilee and laid siege to Tiberias. Within the city were the Countess of Tripoli and her sons.

She wrote to Guy, King of Jerusalem, saying that unless assistance came the place must be surrendered. The Christian forces were gathered at Sefuriyeh some fifteen miles to the west of Tiberias. Raymond, Count of Tripoli, whose wife and children were within the walls, and who therefore had the most to lose, nevertheless counselled that the city should be allowed to fall, " for," he said, " between this place and Tiberias there is not a drop of water. We shall all die of thirst before we get there." The advice was admitted to be sound, and was, at first, accepted. But the Master of the Templars, whose hatred for Raymond knew no bounds, over-persuaded the king to march at once towards Tiberias. To the grief and surprise of the barons the order was given to break up the camp, and the Christian host marched out in silence and sadness to its fate.

The words of Raymond proved only too true. Marching beneath a Syrian summer sun, the wretched Christians were terribly distressed from the heat of the day, the clouds of dust, the burning of the grass beneath their feet by the enemy, and the total absence of water. That night they halted close to the Saracen camp. It was a night of dreadful suffering from want of water. The Saracens, on the other hand, with the Lake of Tiberias at their back had all the water they required. By next morning the Christians had not quenched their thirst for twenty-four hours. With the Christians at so terrible a disadvantage, the battle was lost almost before it commenced. There, at the Horns of Hattin, in one short decisive fight, was settled the fate of the Christian kingdom. No fewer than thirty thousand of the Crusaders are said to have perished on the field. They were completely cowed, demoralized, crushed.

Count Raymond of Tripoli withdrew before the general rout began, and fled to Tyre. King Guy and the Master of the Templars were captured and brought before Saladin. Then was enacted the scene which Sir Walter Scott, adapting the circumstances to the plot of his novel, *The Talisman*, describes so dramatically. The victor presented to his exhausted captive a cup of sherbet cooled in snow. The king having drunk, was about to hand the cup to the Master, when the Sultan interfered. "Your person," he said, "my royal prisoner, is sacred, but the cup of Saladin must not be profaned by a blasphemous robber and ruffian." "The sabre of Saladin left its sheath as lightning leaves the cloud. It was waved in the air, —and the head of the Grand Master rolled to the extremity of the tent, while the trunk remained for a second standing, with the goblet still clenched in its grasp, then fell, the liquor mingling with the blood that spurted from the veins." Thus the Master of the Templars, whose unscrupulous action had precipitated the disaster of the Christians, met with a fate which he thoroughly deserved.

Saladin now set systematically to work to reduce the outlying fortresses and cities, and thus to make himself master of the surrounding country, before turning his face towards Jerusalem. The flower of the Crusaders' army had already been destroyed at the Battle of Hattin, so little opposition was encountered. City after city fell, until only Tyre, Tripoli, and Ascalon remained to the Christians. Ascalon was besieged, and capitulated on terms. Leaving Tyre and Tripoli in the hands of the Christian remnants, Saladin now moved up against Jerusalem. It is noteworthy that the attempt to capture Jerusalem has seldom been made until the conquering army has first possessed itself of the surrounding country on at least three sides. Saladin did but follow the example of Vespasian and Titus.

Saladin now marched upon Jerusalem. On the 20th October, 1187 his army arrived before the western side of the city. Confronted here by a sortie, he moved his army round and set to work to batter the walls on the north. The fighting power of the kingdom having already been spent at Hattin, and there being no hope of the siege being raised from without, the defenders could not be expected to make a stubborn resistance. They offered to capitulate on terms, but Saladin replied that he would capture the city by the sword as the Franks had taken it from "the true believers." The Frank leaders replied that, if terms were not granted, they would sell their lives dearly, destroy the city together with the sacred Mosque of Omar, and murder every Muslim, of whom there were several thousands, within the city. This threat had the desired effect. Terms were arranged; the city was surrendered, and the Christians within were permitted to depart on payment of ransom.

The fall of Jerusalem caused a thrill of consternation throughout Europe. So long as the tottering kingdom remained, Europe turned a deaf ear to her appeals. But now that the kingdom had been overthrown, and the Moslem was actually in possession of the Holy Sepulchre, Europe awoke, reproached herself for her supineness, and the old Crusading enthusiasm flashed out anew. This time the adherence was secured of no less than three sovereign monarchs who took the cross and raised armies for the expedition to Palestine, the Emperor of Germany, and the Kings respectively of England and of France. This, the Third Crusade, is the one most familiar to Englishmen from its association with the English King, Richard Cœur de Lion.

The Germans were the first to start. They followed the route of previous crusades across Europe and Asia Minor, with much the same result. So greatly were their ranks thinned on the way by fighting and pestilence, that only a very few of these reached Syria. The other parties, profiting by the unfortunate experiences of previous crusades, came by sea, the English from Marseilles and the French from Genoa.

We have seen that, after the fall of Jerusalem, Tyre, to which city Raymond had resorted from the disastrous battlefield of Hattin, still remained in the hands of the Christians. After settling the affairs of captured Jerusalem, Saladin moved to

Acre and made preparations for the siege of Tyre. His operations for the capture of that city having proved unsuccessful, he withdrew first to Acre, and then away northwards. The Christians in Tyre took heart at this withdrawal, and, strengthened by the arrival of the first party of the Third Crusaders, they set out in July, 1189, to lay siege to Acre. The siege of this town proved a lengthy business, as the town was well garrisoned and provisioned. Saladin marched rapidly south and settled down within a few miles of the Christians. A kind of double siege followed, the Christian army besieging Acre, and Saladin's army besieging the Christians. As the French and English contingents of the Third Crusade reached Palestine by sea, they arrived opportunely to take part in this siege of Acre. By the summer of 1191 the strength of the Christian army had been raised to more than a hundred thousand, and the siege was pressed with vigour. In July of that year the garrison surrendered. The French king then returned home, and the undivided command devolved upon King Richard. A garrison was left at Acre, and then the Crusading army set out upon its southward march towards Jerusalem. Richard moved along the coastal plain, by way of Cæsarea. The Moslems moved parallel but further inland, their cavalry using the cover of the olive groves for ambushes and skirmishes. At Arsuf, some nine miles north of Jaffa, a pitched battle was fought, in which complete success lay with the Crusaders. But this success was not followed up. Richard moved instead to Jaffa, and there prepared deliberately for the expedition against Jerusalem.

Saladin decided that the forces at his disposal were not sufficient for the defence of both Ascalon and Jerusalem. He therefore abandoned Ascalon, the fortifications of which he demolished. After ensuring that Jerusalem was in a complete state of readiness to withstand a siege, and having demolished Ramleh and Ludd upon the Plain, he withdrew his army into the foothills at Latron.

The winter was spent in inactivity, the Crusaders at Jaffa, the Moslem army at Latron. Negotiations were carried on between Richard and Saladin, both of whom hoped to attain their objectives if possible without fighting. The negotiations proved abortive. In the spring of 1192 the war recommenced. Instead of marching at once upon Jerusalem, the goal of the campaign, Richard despatched a force southwards. This force captured Gaza, and also Darum, a fortress situated beyond Gaza on the border of the Egyptian territory. A strong Saracen force had been raised in Egypt to assist Saladin and to relieve the anticipated siege of Jerusalem. This force marched up out of Egypt, and the Crusaders lay in wait. The Egyptian force encamped for the night by El Khaweilifeh not far from Gaza, where they were completely surprised and routed. The Crusaders had thus secured two undoubted successes, but they were still no nearer the capture of the Holy City.

King Richard decided that the time had now come for the advance upon Jerusalem. (As a matter of fact the time had come immediately after the battle of Arsuf; now it had long since passed.) Richard therefore moved his force up into the hills not far from Bab el Wad on the road from Jaffa to Jerusalem. Here he vacillated. The ever-recurring question of water raised his apprehensions. He could not make up his mind. One day he rode within sight of the city. Bursting into tears, and covering his face with his shield, he cried aloud that he was not worthy even to look upon the city of his Saviour. Dissensions broke out between King Richard and the Duke of Burgundy. The design of besieging Jerusalem was abandoned, and slowly and sadly the army returned through Ramleh to Jaffa.

After an unsuccessful expedition by the Crusaders against Beirut, and an equally unsuccessful expedition by Saladin against Jaffa, the operations reached a condition of stalemate. It was clear that the Crusaders could not capture Jerusalem;

it was equally clear that the Moslems could not drive them from the country. Accordingly a truce was agreed to, which ripened into a treaty, for arms were not again taken up by Richard or Saladin. By this truce the littoral from Jaffa to Cæsarea and from Acre to Tyre was to remain in the hands of the Crusaders. Ludd and Ramleh were to be considered common gound. The Crusaders were given free access to Jerusalem, taking advantage of which they visited the Holy Sepulchre in crowds. Richard, deciding to return to his neglected kingdom of England, embarked for Europe in October, 1192, leaving the Holy Land for ever. Saladin, after touring through Syria organizing its good government, returned to Damascus. But his rest was short-lived, for within but a few months this greatest of Saracens lay dead.

The Third Crusade had failed in its primary objects, the recapture of Jerusalem and the restoration to its capital of the decadent kingdom of the Crusaders. It had so far succeeded, however, that it had enabled the remnants of that kingdom, not only to retain their foothold, but to considerably strengthen their precarious position in the Holy Land. That position, through endless vicissitudes, continued for yet another century.

The Christian kingdom now consisted of a strip of territory along the coast, with its capital at Acre. Here the titular king of Jerusalem held sway. But the magnet, which had previously drawn pilgrims from all over Christendom to the armies of the cross, had ceased to attract. The kingdom, such as it was, owed its continued existence to the military orders of the Knights.

There were several subsequent Crusades, most of which never even reached the Holy Land. None of them made any pretence of conquering Palestine or ranked in magnitude with the first three. One was directed against the Moslem power in Egypt where it failed ignominiously. One was wholly diverted in the interests of Venice to effecting the conquest

THE CRUSADES

of their fellow-Christians at Constantinople. Strangest and most pathetic of all was the Children's Crusade. It was a popular opinion—one might almost say superstition—that the failure of the Crusaders to retain or regain the Holy City was entirely due to the wickedness of the Crusaders themselves, and that if only an army could be raised which would be wholly blameless, however deficient in military ability, the Almighty would most certainly deliver into their hands the Holy City and the Sepulchre of Christ. In the year 1212 priests went about France and Germany preaching a crusade and calling upon children to rally to the cross and to achieve that wherein their fathers had failed. Thousands of children of both sexes responded to the call. Enthusiasm spread like an epidemic. Despite the frantic endeavours of their parents to restrain them, the children broke loose and rushed to join the throng. They had no money, no provisions, and no leaders, depending wholly upon the charity of the towns through which they passed. They marched in two columns. One column of these poor little children trudged through Germany, and across the Alps, waving their flags, singing their hymns, and suffering untold privations. A remnant of this band, about seven thousand strong, mostly robbed and debauched, at length reached Genoa. Here they expected to find some miraculous means of reaching the Holy Land. But mercifully for them no such miracle occurred. Disappointed and disheartened they broke up; those that were fortunate at last regained their homes, but with hearts broken and faith shattered. The fate of the children who went through France was yet more sad. They made their way to Marseilles. Here they found two merchants, traders with the East, who had then in port several ships lying empty. Generously espousing their cause, these merchants offered the poor children a free passage to the Holy Land. Delighted at this apparent miracle, the children sailed away in high glee. But, alas, the destination of these poor Innocents was not the Holy Sepulchre, but the slave markets of Alexandria,—thence to finish their miserable existence in the brothels of the East.

In the year A.D. 1244 there was verily and indeed another conquest of Palestine. This time it came neither from Crusader nor from Moslem. Regardless of both, the Kharezmian Tartars swept down from Central Asia and carried all before them. They butchered Moslem and Christian without discrimination. The Templars at Acre called on the Saracen princes of Damascus and other towns to join with them against the common enemy. The Saracens responded to the call. They met the Kharezmians on the Plain of Philistia, but were defeated. The destruction committed by the Kharezmians throughout the land was such as to surpass many even of the previous ravages. Eventually the Sultan of Cairo sent an army of Egyptians against them. The Kharezmians were defeated in several battles, and driven from the country, disappearing from the face of history as suddenly as they had appeared.

The coalition of Moslem and Christian in the face of common danger stands out as one of the few bright spots in the sordid history of the Crusades. The final act in this drama was played in 1291. The Moslem army of the Egyptian Mameluke Sultan captured their last stronghold, Acre, and the Crusaders were finally expelled from Palestine.

CHAPTER X

THE FRENCH

AFTER the expulsion of the Crusaders from Palestine, the country continued under the sway of the Mameluke Sultans of Egypt. In A.D. 1400 the country was overrun by Timur the Tartar (Tamberlane), who did not however succeed in permanently overthrowing the Mamelukes. The end of their sovereignty came with the rise of the Ottoman Turks. The extension of the Ottoman empire throughout Asia Minor and across the Hellespont into Europe was the outcome of a gradual expansion extending over some centuries. More than half a century had already elapsed since the capture of Constantinople, when, in the sixteenth century A.D., the Ottomans sought to include Syria, Palestine and Egypt in their empire. The Turks under Selim the Grim were operating against Persia, when the Mameluke Sultan of Cairo, apprehensive of danger, posted an army of observation on the Syrian frontier. This Selim construed as a menace, and decided upon war against the Mamelukes. Setting out for Syria in A.D. 1516, Selim met the Mameluke army near Aleppo, where he administered a terrible defeat in which the Mameluke Sultan was killed. The Turks soon mastered Syria and advanced to Gaza. Here the Mamelukes made another attempt to stop their advance, but without success. The final battle was fought near Cairo, consequent upon which Egypt, and with it also Palestine and Syria, passed under the Ottoman Porte.

In the course of the next three hundred years great changes

passed over the Ottoman Empire. By the end of the eighteenth century many of the Turkish provinces were in open revolt against the Sultan, chief of which was Egypt, where the Mamelukes still formed a complete military oligarchy. The rule of the Porte had been represented in Egypt by a Pasha, but with the decline of the Sultan's power, the authority of his Pasha in Egypt had declined also. The Mamelukes chose their own leader, reduced the Turkish garrison at Cairo, and sent the Pasha back to the Porte. This revolutionary action of the Mamelukes was used by the French in 1798 as an excuse for their invasion of Egypt. They then gave out that they were coming to Egypt to overthrow the Mamelukes and restore the Sultan; but the hollowness of the excuse was too palpable to deceive anybody, least of all the Sultan.

Napoleon Bonaparte, having completed his victorious campaign in Italy, had returned in triumph to Paris. Employment had now to be found for him and his armies, while the Directory in Paris were anxious to keep him at a distance from the capital. Accordingly the plan was conceived of invading Egypt. Besides serving its immediate purposes of keeping Napoleon at a distance and his armies occupied, such a campaign offered some promise of checkmating France's principal enemy, England. Moreover Napoleon dreamed of an empire in the East, rivalling that of Alexander. Visions of a push through to India to assist their ally Tippoo Sahib in his struggles against Wellesley, or of a victorious return to France by way of Asia Minor and Constantinople, both crossed the horizon of Napoleon's imagination.

Towards the middle of May, 1798, Napoleon embarked with an army at Toulon for a secret destination. So close was the secret kept that Nelson, who lay in wait, was ordered to take particular care to prevent the French convoy from passing through the Straits of Gibraltar to Ireland. Eluding the British fleet, the French Navy proceeded to Malta, which was surrendered without a shot. Thence they passed on to Egypt, and the French army had already disembarked at Marabout near Alexandria and marched away to the South, before Nelson had discovered their whereabouts.

Marching along the Nile, Napoleon came within sight of the Pyramids at Gizeh, immediately opposite Cairo. Murad the Mameluke leader collected the bulk of his forces at the village of Embabeh, and, ignorant or contemptuous of the military power that had come against him, played into the hands of the invader. " Soldats ! " cried Napoleon addressing his men, " songez que du haut de ces monuments quarante siècles vous contemplent." The opposing forces joined combat. On July 21st, 1798, the Mameluke chivalry fought and lost their last great battle. Half of them fled into Upper Egypt, half into Syria, leaving Napoleon to enter Cairo in triumph.

Meanwhile the British fleet, which had been searching around the Mediterranean for the elusive Frenchmen, had found them at last lying in Aboukir Bay, a few miles to the east of Alexandria. Action was joined at once, and on the 1st August, little more than a week after Napoleon's victory at the Battle of the Pyramids, his fleet was destroyed at the Battle of the Nile.

Napoleon's communications with France were thus severed at an early stage of his enterprise. Nevertheless his army was, to a great extent, self-supporting. In a fertile country like Egypt, the loss of communication by sea did not immediately involve serious consequences. Napoleon at once took steps to make good his position in Egypt, while the scientists that he had brought with him from France improvised factories for gunpowder and other requisites for war.

The Ottoman Porte were not deceived by Napoleon's plausible excuse that he was fighting the Mamelukes in the interests of the Turks. They at once declared war against the French and set about the preparation of expeditions to drive them out of Egypt. Two Turkish armies were organized. One, based on Rhodes, was to land on the coast of Egypt; the other, based on Damascus, was to advance through Palestine.

Bonaparte, ever ready to assume the offensive, decided to strike the enemy in Syria before his organization was complete, and then return to Egypt in time to deal with the army from Rhodes. Preparations were pushed forward at his base, Katia, a little to the north-east of Kantara. The water problem was to some extent minimised by the fact that the advance was to be made in February. Nevertheless each mounted man carried with him two gallons of water, while three extra gallons were carried with each cavalry section.

The advance commenced on the 7th February, 1799, and by the 20th El Arish had been reached and captured. Thence the advance was continued through Khan Yunus to Gaza. At this place there were large supply and ammunition dumps, but the Turks surrendered it without a fight. Thus, the dreaded desert passed, Napoleon was able to turn Gaza into a base for a fresh advance into the fertile plains of Syria.

Esdud and Ramleh having been occupied, Jaffa became the next objective. Siege was laid to this place, which was captured by assault on the 6th March, the whole garrison over four thousand strong falling into the hands of the French. Between two and three thousand prisoners had surrendered, on condition that their lives should be spared. Faced with the difficulty of disposing of these prisoners, for whom Napoleon could afford neither food nor escorts, he had them all murdered in cold blood upon the beach.

Pushing on northwards, the next objective was Acre. Haifa, which had been abandoned by the Turks, was occupied and garrisoned, and a systematic siege was laid to Acre. Screens were thrown out, as far as Tyre on the north, Safed on the east, and Nazareth on the south-east, in order to protect the besieging army from outside interference. But the command of the sea, which had been secured by the British at the Battle of the Nile, proved invaluable. A British squadron cruising off the Syrian coast had intercepted and captured seven French vessels which were bringing up several 24-pounder siege guns intended for use against Acre. The squadron moved up to Acre, where men and guns were landed. Sir Sydney Smith, the commander, at once set about putting the defences in order. When the British arrived, the only guns mounted were a few looking seawards; on the landward side the defences were but slight, and the captured French siege guns therefore proved a useful addition.

Meanwhile the Turkish army from Damascus was moving forward against Napoleon. Accordingly he left a small force to watch Acre, sent General Murat to deal with a small portion of the enemy force which was on the march towards Safed, and took the bulk of his army to deal with the main force of the Turks which had crossed the Jordan south of the Sea of Galilee and was marching on Tiberias. This Turkish force, some twenty to thirty thousand strong, was concentrating by the Plain of Esdraelon between Mount Tabor and El Fule. Moving upon them from the direction of Nazareth, Napoleon completely routed them in the battle of Mount Tabor, and drove them back across the Jordan. Thus one of Napoleon's objectives, the crushing of the main Turkish army in Syria, had been accomplished.

Napoleon returned to the siege of Acre. Hitherto more initiative had been shown by the besieged than by the besiegers; the number of the sallies exceeded that of the assaults. Operations were now pressed with greater vigour; but, in spite of repeated and determined assaults, the town continued to resist. After the last assault Sydney Smith informed the Home Authorities that he feared that Acre could not withstand another attack. But on the 20th May Napoleon, despairing of taking the town and with pressing reasons for an early return to Egypt, raised the siege and withdrew southwards, thus abandoning his dreams of an empire in the East or a return to Europe through Constantinople. In later years he is reported to have said

"Had Acre fallen, I should have changed the face of the world."

Napoleon returned to Egypt along much the same route as that by which he had advanced. Every village on the line of retreat had been destroyed and the crops burnt. Crossing the desert, now in the heat of June, his troops suffered terribly from thirst, while his difficulties were further increased by the large number of his men who were stricken with plague. Cairo was reached on the 21st June.

The return of Napoleon and the remnants of his army to Egypt was only just in time for them to prepare for the Turkish army which had been organized at Rhodes to invade Egypt by sea. This Turkish army landed at Aboukir. Napoleon instantly marched for the coast, won a brilliant victory, and drove back the Turks. But all hope of attaining an empire in the East had gone, so Napoleon now abandoned his army in Egypt, embarked from Alexandria on the 25th August, 1799, and returned to France, there to become Dictator and undertake fresh campaigns of conquest in the West. The command of the French army left in Egypt was taken over by Kleber. In 1801 a British expedition was sent out under Sir Ralph Abercrombie to expel the French from Egypt by force. This expedition landed at Aboukir, and defeated the French. Terms were eventually arranged, under which the French evacuated Egypt, and were allowed to march out with all the honours of war, being granted a safe convoy to France.

Thus closed the French invasion of Egypt and Palestine. Though short-lived, it had a more lasting sequel. With the Turkish armies that came to Egypt at this time, was an Albanian volunteer or Bashi-Bazouk, by name Mehemet Ali. When the British evacuated Egypt in 1803, the question arose as to who should govern there in future. The Turks wished to restore their pashalik after thirty years' abeyance, and the Mamelukes hoped to revive their supremacy as it existed prior to Napoleon's invasion. The Albanian element, of which

Mehemet Ali had become head, to some extent held aloof from both parties. Playing his hand with consummate skill and seizing his opportunity, Mehemet Ali threw in his lot with the Turkish party and in 1805 had himself proclaimed Pasha of Egypt. He advanced his authority by stages; but his actions were much encumbered, and his ambitions thwarted, by the presence of the turbulent and hostile Mamelukes. In 1811 Mehemet Ali, by a coup d'état, entrapped the Mamelukes in the Citadel at Cairo and had them massacred to a man. With the Mamelukes removed from his path, Mehemet Ali was able to make such strides that in a short space he was virtually dictator of Egypt. He superseded his wild Albanian soldiers with newly raised and well-trained regiments of Soudanese and Egyptian fellaheen. But he was playing for a yet higher stake. In 1831, he despatched an expedition under his son Ibrahim, which advanced through Syria and into Asia Minor, where the forces of his old master, the Sultan of Turkey, were defeated at the battle of Konia.

Mehemet Ali was now at the zenith of his power. He overreached himself however. His administration of Syria proved even worse than had been that of the Turks, and all Syria soon revolted against his tyranny. A small Turkish force, with a European stiffening attacked and captured Acre from the sea, and Ibrahim was forced to withdraw into Egypt.

With the consent of the European Powers, Mehemet Ali and his successors became hereditary rulers of Egypt, with virtually absolute power, subject to the nominal suzerainty of Turkey. Syria resumed its place in the Ottoman Empire.

CHAPTER XI

THE BRITISH

THE invasion of Palestine by the British in 1917 was undertaken primarily in the defence of Egypt. Before considering in detail this, the last campaign in Palestine, it is necessary therefore to trace the leading events in the history of Egypt, following the establishment of Mehemet Ali and his successors as hereditary rulers.

The most important event in this period was the construction, and opening in 1869, of the Suez Canal. Although the property of a French Company, its maintenance has always been of even more importance to Great Britain. Through it passes the bulk of the shipping plying between Great Britain and her possessions in the East. It is the high road to India, and has been aptly described as " the main artery of the British Empire."

Thus it was to the interest of Europe in general, and of France and more especially of Britain in particular, that Egypt should henceforth be firmly and ably governed and the Suez Canal adequately defended. In 1863 Mehemet Ali's grandson, Ismail, had become Khedive of Egypt. The financial policy of Ismail was little short of hopeless. By reckless borrowing and prodigal expenditure he soon reduced the exchequer to a condition of chaos. No alternative remained but European intervention. This intervention was followed by a wave of Anti-European feeling throughout the country, in consequence of which the discontented army, headed by Arabi

Pasha, rose in 1882 in open revolt against the Khedive and government.

A crisis had now been reached; and the time for armed intervention had arrived. Combined action by France and Britain was contemplated, but at the last moment the French withdrew, leaving the British with a free hand. In consequence of riots and massacres of Europeans which occurred at Alexandria, the forts there were bombarded and a small force was landed to restore order. An expedition was then sent up the Suez Canal and disembarked at Ismailia. Marching thence towards Cairo, it met and defeated the Egyptian army in the one and only battle of the campaign at Tel-el-Kebir. Arabi had been overthrown, and the Khedive was restored to power. But now arose a dilemma. The British had not come with the intention of remaining in Egypt. If, on the other hand, they had withdrawn, the country would have been left again at the mercy of the insurgents. No course remained open therefore but for the British army to remain in occupation. The British occupation of Egypt, which thus commenced in 1882, has remained to the present day.

With the military occupation of the country, the British also took over the financial, industrial, and civil control, mainly in an advisory capacity, but not the less effectually. Except for the two Soudanese wars, a reign of settled peace and prosperity was enjoyed. Incidentally Britain was thus in a position to ensure the adequate defence of the Suez Canal.

It was in August, 1914, that the great war cloud burst upon Europe. The ostensible cause was the intention of Austria to punish Serbia for the murder of a member of the Austrian Royal house. In reality it was the determination of Germany, allied with Austria, to humiliate France and Russia. Very soon half Europe was involved, Great Britain coming in immediately upon the side of France.

At the onset of the war Europe was kept in suspense as to the intentions of Turkey. Her control of the Dardanelles would have made her a useful ally to the Franco-British. But German propaganda had recently been busy in that country, and when the only two German warships in the Mediterranean fled to Constantinople for refuge, signs were becoming fairly evident as to the side which Turkey intended to join. At the end of October Turkey definitely entered the war on the side of Austria and Germany, and against France and Britain.

Foremost among the inducements held out by Germany to the Porte, to secure its adherence, was the promise that Turkey should be restored to complete power in Egypt, instead of the merely nominal suzerainty which she had held since the days of Mehemet Ali. On Turkey declaring war, the British at once repudiated the Turkish suzerainty and declared Egypt to be a British Protectorate.

It was to be expected that Germany would make some show of fulfilling her promise to Turkey, and would embark upon an expedition with the combined object, of restoring the Turks to Egypt, and of cutting "the main artery of the British Empire."

Measures were accordingly pushed on with for the defence of the Suez Canal. Portions of the low-lying country on the east of the Canal were flooded, gun-boats took up stations in the lakes, and troops were concentrated along the western bank. The line of the Canal thus became the line of resistance, not only for the defence of Egypt but also for the defence of the Canal itself. Behind lay the fertile delta, good roads and railways, and an abundant supply of fresh water. In front lay a hundred miles of waterless almost impassable desert. The defensive line at first sight seemed ideal.

The Turks did not allow the grass to grow under their feet, but soon organized an Army in Syria for the invasion of Egypt. They constructed a new railway from the Haifa line to Beersheba and out into the desert, thus establishing railway communication, by way of Damascus, with Asia Minor. Aided by the Germans they pushed across the desert dragging with them their artillery, and, in April 1915, they delivered an attack against the Suez Canal. With them they had brought several light steel pontoons, which they launched upon the Canal and in which they endeavoured to effect a crossing. These came under a furious rifle and machine gun fire from the troops posted on the western bank. The few Turks who effected a landing were unsupported and therefore surrendered. British troops were pushed across the Canal and a counter-attack was delivered. The Turks were defeated, and eventually withdrew across the desert into Syria.

For the remainder of the year attention was diverted from Egypt by the British attempt to force the passage of the Dardanelles and carry the war to the gates of Constantinople. Whilst this expedition was in progress all available Turkish troops were concentrated in defence of the capital and no further invasion of Egypt was attempted. With the withdrawal of the British force from Gallipoli and the abandonment of the Dardanelles expedition at the end of the year, the flower of the Turkish army was again released and a further invasion of Egypt was to be expected.

Now although the former attempt at invading Egypt had proved a failure, it had opened the eyes of the British to certain vulnerable spots in their line of defence. The western bank of the Canal, with the Canal used as a moat, had proved an excellent line on which to defend Egypt; but it had proved an unsatisfactory line on which to defend the Canal itself. It left the enemy free to approach within artillery range, to bombard the passing traffic, and surreptitiously to sow mines in the fairway. Some better line had to be found for the future defence of the Canal. A line pushed out into the desert would suffice as a temporary measure; but to keep a garrison stretched out across the desert for all time was out of the question. It was therefore necessary to seek a line further to the east, clear of the desert, that is to say, in Palestine.

The advantages which an invasion of Palestine offered to

the British may be summed up as follows. It would enable them to secure a satisfactory line of defence for the Suez Canal. On the principle that the best defensive is a vigorous offensive, it would protect Egypt from further invasion. It would carry the war into the enemy's country. And, finally, in co-operation with other armies of the allies operating in Asiatic Turkey, it would strike at the strategic centre of the Eastern theatres of war and might culminate in the rounding up of the whole Turkish army in Asia.

Early in 1916 accordingly a new line was taken up as a temporary measure, and consolidated with trenches and barbed wire, in the desert some ten miles to the east of the canal. Kantara, situated where the caravan route from Africa into Asia crosses the Canal, was developed into a great base. Construction was commenced of the two achievements of modern engineering which were to solve the problems of transport and water. The former was met by the construction of a substantial broad gauge railway. For the latter a piped service was installed, whereby water, brought by the Sweet Water Canal from the Nile to Kantara, was pumped forward in successive stages across the desert, until at length it was being delivered into the British trenches before Gaza.

As the construction of the railway and pipe line permitted, so the British position was pushed eastwards out into the desert. The advance was not allowed to proceed however unmolested. The British withdrawal from the Dardanelles having released the Turkish armies, they came pouring down into Asia. A second Turkish advance was now made across the desert with the object of countering British activity, and, if successful, of pushing on again towards Egypt. A battle was fought at Romani in the desert, in which the Turks were worsted. Thenceforward the initiative passed from their hands, and their subsequent activities were devoted merely to countering the activities of the British. Throughout that summer the British advance was slowly but steadily continued across the desert and by Christmas 1916 El Arish had been reached. Near here some minor engagements were fought against the retreating Turkish rearguards, after which the Turks took up a position at Gaza with a portion of their force near Beersheba.

Gaza, the outpost of Africa, the gate of Asia, has been taken and destroyed in war more often probably than any other city in the world. It was the scene of no less than three bloody battles before the British could push past it into Palestine. The first was fought in March 1917. The British troops which had concentrated at Rafa, were marched up by night. In the early morning, in dense fog that hampered the operations, they found themselves approaching Gaza. Their main objective, the commanding hill Ali Muntar, was captured without great difficulty, the cavalry got all round the town, and the Turks were on the point of surrendering. Meanwhile, Turkish reinforcements had been ordered to move across from Beersheba. Fearing that these would fall upon the flank of the British or cut their communications, the British commander ordered a retreat ; Gaza was evacuated ; and the force fell back across the Wadi Ghuzzeh to Deir el Belah.

The Turks now set assiduously to work preparing a strong line of entrenchments with barbed wire entanglements, in readiness for the next attempt. They had not long to wait. In the middle of April the British moved forward again. They endeavoured to apply the new method of trench to trench warfare which had recently been learnt on the battlefields of France. The newly invented " tanks," which were expected to carry all before them, broke down, or blew up. The sixty minutes preparatory bombardment of the Turkish trenches ceased in sufficient time to enable the enemy machine guns to come into action and to mow down the infantry advancing across the open. When darkness fell, the Turkish positions had not been captured, and all there was to show as the result of a day's fighting was a glacis slope strewn with dead and dying British. Under cover of darkness those who could do so crept back to the cover of the ridge from which the advance had been launched. Here they joined the reserves and a line was hastily entrenched. The Turks showed no disposition to follow up their success with a determined counter-attack, and so the British were allowed to consolidate a line within a thousand yards or so of Gaza.

Throughout the summer of 1917 the armies sat facing each other in their trenches at Gaza. The normal state of trench warfare, with its daily shelling, nightly patrolling, and periodical raiding, prevailed. The British army was strongly reinforced; General Allenby, who had distinguished himself in France, was sent out and took over command. By the end of October his preparations were complete, and he was ready to fight the third great battle of Gaza.

The Turkish position consisted of a strong line based on Gaza and Beersheba. On its right flank it rested upon the sea; on the left was a waterless desert. The defensive works consisted of the main position at Gaza, which had been converted into an almost impregnable modern fortress. Except for a gap of a thousand yards near, and commanded by, Ali Muntar, an almost continuous line of trenches ran south-east along the Gaza-Beersheba road as far as Sheria. There was an interval of five miles, and then another system of trenches around Beersheba, protecting the important wells in that town, and serving as a strong outwork to the left flank of the Gaza-Sheria trench system.

General Allenby decided to deliver his main attack against the left flank of the Sheria position; the operations in other quarters of the battlefield were to be subordinate. The first operation was the capture of the Beersheba position, providing an ample water supply and exposing the flank of the Turkish position at Sheria. Then, at the other end of the line, followed an attack upon the Gaza position by the shore, the Navy co-operating with a bombardment from the sea. This operation had the desired effect of pinning the garrison of Gaza to their positions and preventing their withdrawal to reinforce Sheria; it also had the effect of drawing into Gaza, and thus using up, a portion of the Turkish reserves. Then, finally, was delivered the main attack against the position at Sheria. All the operations were successful. They extended over a period of nine days; the capture of Beersheba was effected on October 31 and by November 8 the broken Turkish force was in full retreat.

The pursuit was now taken up by as many troops as could be supplied at a distance from railhead. A few of the enemy retired into the hills towards Hebron, but the majority fled northwards along the coastal plain. The next point of tactical importance was the Junction Station, where the railway line to Jerusalem leaves that from the north to Beersheba. By the 13th the Turks had rallied on a line distant about five miles from, and covering, this point. In their semi-disorganized state they were unable to offer any very stout resistance here, their flank was easily turned, and they were driven back again in disorder. Junction Station fell into the hands of the British, while the broken Turkish army retired, part of it eastwards towards Jerusalem, and part of it northwards through Ludd and Ramleh towards Tul Keram. The British occupied Jaffa.

The Turks being now on the run, it was decided to push forward at once and endeavour to capture Jerusalem. The force moved eastward in parallel columns, part moving up from Ramleh along the valley of Ajalon and part from Junction Station through Latron and up the main Jerusalem road. The objective which it was hoped to capture was Bireh, a high commanding position a few miles to the north of Jerusalem. Accordingly no immediate attempt was made to reach the Holy City itself, but a line was struck across the mountains in an east-north-easterly direction. It was found impossible to bring forward artillery; stubborn Turkish resistance was encountered; and the project of reaching Bireh immediately proved to be out of the question. On November 21 a commanding position was captured known as Neby Samwil. This, the Mizpeh of the Bible, and the birth and burial place of the prophet Samuel, proved to be the key of Jerusalem. Fierce and desperate was the fighting around this spot. Nevertheless this captured position was held, though further advance was for the time being impossible. The line was consolidated, and the mountain tracks were converted as rapidly as possible into roads good enough for the bringing up of artillery. Operations for the capture of Jerusalem were renewed on December 8. A wheeling advance was made, pivoting on Neby Samwil. In this way it was possible to get astride the two main roads leading into Jerusalem on the north and west. Meanwhile a division, that had been left behind at Beersheba, marched northward along the hill road by way of Hebron and Bethlehem, and at the crucial moment got astride the two main roads leading into Jerusalem on the south and east. The city was now completely cut off and on December 9 it surrendered.

Thus again, after more than seven centuries, was Jerusalem entered by a Christian conqueror. Not a stone of the city had been injured. The lives, liberty and property of the inhabitants were scrupulously respected. Not a soldier was allowed to enter the city, except on duty, until all the sacred spots had been placed under guards, consisting of men of the religions to which such spots were respectively sacred.

Having thus reached a definite stage in the history of the British invasion, we must turn aside for a few moments to consider two related campaigns which were then in progress and which, from this time forward, excercised considerable influence on the campaign in which we are more closely interested.

On the outbreak of the war with Turkey the British landed a force at the head of the Persian Gulf. This force, with varying fortunes, fought its way up into Mesopotamia. By March 1917 it had reached and captured Baghdad. Still pushing forward up the valleys of the Tigris and Euphrates, it gradually cleared away the remaining Turkish garrisons and continued to menace a further advance towards Mosul. The main Turkish line of communications from Constantinople and Europe to Mesopotamia passed through Aleppo; as far as that centre the lines of communications to Mesopotamia and to Palestine were identical. Thus the Turks were able to form a strategic reserve at Aleppo capable of being rapidly moved to either front. The British operations in Mesopotamia may to some extent have assisted those in Palestine by drawing Turkish reserves in that direction, but it is probable that, by drawing Turkish reserves into Palestine, the British operations in that country more materially assisted the later stages of the invasion of Mesopotamia.

The other campaign lay in the Hejaz. In June 1916 the Sheriff of Mecca rose in rebellion against the Turks. Although of the same religion, the Arabs possessed little in common with their Turkish masters, and were glad of the opportunity, afforded by Turkey's embarrassments in other fields of war, to rise in revolt. Medina was besieged and masked. All the other Turkish troops in the country were captured. The Arab army gradually advanced up the line of the Hejaz railway by way of Maan and the east of the Dead Sea. From the capture of Jerusalem onwards this Arab army was able to exercise not a little influence on the British campaign in Palestine, while at the final battle their co-operation east of the Jordan proved invaluable.

We return now to the British army which we left in recent possession of Jerusalem. After a pause of a couple of months for consolidation, and to allow the worst of the weather to pass by, forward movement was resumed in February, 1918. Jericho was captured without much difficulty and a steady advance northwards of a few miles was made by the whole line across Palestine from the sea to the Jordan Valley. An attempt to break through the centre of the Turkish line, made in

March and April, only failed through the sudden depletion of the British forces in Palestine, in order to save the situation in France.

In March, 1918, the German army broke through the Franco-British line in France. Orders were sent for the despatch from Palestine immediately of all possible British troops, and the temporary cessation of active hostilities on this front. Accordingly there was no alternative but to consolidate the line already gained, and to withdraw a very large number of British units and replace them with newly raised battalions of Indians. Two partially successful raids were however carried out across the Jordan, against the Hejaz railway.

By the following September General Allenby was ready for his last and crowning battle. The Turkish line stretched across Palestine from the sea near Arsuf, some ten miles north of Jaffa, to the Jordan Valley. The Turks knew that an attack was imminent, but were ignorant as to the exact spot at which it would be delivered. Accordingly every expedient was used to convey the impression that an attack was to be delivered up the Jordan Valley. By moving troops at night, and hiding them in the orange and olive groves by day, an overwhelming force was concentrated and concealed behind the British front line upon the coastal plain.

The blow fell in the early morning of September 19. The British line from Rafat, in the hills, to the sea swung round through a quarter of a circle with a radius of about sixteen miles. The Turks were taken completely by surprise, and their line rolled up. By the next morning the whole Turkish army west of the Jordan, surrounded and cut off, was fleeing, a panic-stricken rabble, into the arms of the British cavalry.

The battle was continued for the next two or three days. Another expedition was sent across the Jordan, which, with the aid of the Arabs, accounted for the Turkish army east of the river. Then ensued a race for Damascus. The Turks had a few reserve troops there, which they sent down to the crossing of the Jordan north of Lake Tiberias, and tried to hold up the British advance at that point. The opposition was brushed aside and, without much further fighting, Damascus was captured. Place after place in Northern Syria fell before the advancing cavalry and armoured cars, until by the end of October the British and Arabs had occupied Aleppo.

The conquest of Palestine and Syria was complete. The war with Turkey was ended. On October 31, 1918, an armistice came into force by which Turkey virtually surrendered unconditionally. A few weeks later the European powers concluded an armistice, and the greatest war in the history of the world was at an end.

CHAPTER XII

CONCLUSION

WE have passed in review the more important of the many campaigns that have swept over Palestine in the course of four thousand years. Though widely divergent in date, we have been struck by many similarities of motive and of plan of campaign. In some the impelling motive has been strategical, in some, religious. In some the main objective has been Jerusalem, while in some the capture of that city has been a mere incident or has been wholly ignored.

Although different motives often co-existed and overlapped, yet we may attempt a rough analysis of the sundry motives which influenced these various campaigns. Throughout our review, strategical wars have been the most common. Into that category fall the wars of the Egyptians, Assyrians, Babylonians, Greeks, French and British. The Crusades on the other hand were primarily religious. Religion and colonization together furnished pretexts to the Jews and to the Arabs. Extension of empire alone seems to have brought the Romans and the Turks to Palestine. Rapine and murder attracted most of the invaders, but especially the Persians and Tartars.

A few words here may not be out of place with reference to the religious attraction of Jerusalem, round which so much strife has centred. From the earliest times some degree of sanctity seems to have attached to this spot. Strong tradition fixes Mount Moriah as that on which Abraham was about to sacrifice Isaac. But the sacredness of the City of Jerusalem

CONCLUSION

became more pronounced after its capture by David, the removal thither of the Ark of the Covenant, and the erection of the Temple. We have only to read Solomon's dedication prayer, with his request that all prayers thenceforth offered to God with face towards the temple should be more abundantly blessed, to understand how Jerusalem then became, and has ever since remained, the sacred city of the Jew.

A thousand years later and Jesus Christ is born at Bethlehem, within a few miles of Jerusalem. In Jerusalem itself were performed many of His wonderful works, here did He preach and teach, here did He suffer and was crucified, died and was buried and the third day rose again according to the scriptures and ascended into Heaven. Thus did Jerusalem become, and has ever since remained, the sacred city of the Christian.

Another interval of six centuries and Mahomet stands forth as the Prophet of God. The religion which he founded and taught was based upon Judaism and Christianity. Following Solomon, he at first commanded the faithful to turn themselves in prayer towards Jerusalem; it was only in consequence of the estrangement with the Jews that he afterwards substituted Mecca. All faithful Moslems believe that the Prophet was borne by the angel Gabriel on a winged steed from Mecca to Jerusalem and that from Mount Moriah he then ascended to Heaven. They also believe that at Jerusalem, and not at Mecca, Medina or elsewhere upon the earth, is to be the Plain of Marshalling on the Day of Judgment. Thus is Jerusalem no less a city sacred to the Moslem.

The problem of reconciling all these religions in one city is not easy. When the Jew was in power he rigorously excluded the Gentile from the Temple. When the Moslem came into power, he as rigorously excluded the Jew. The contending sects of Christianity cannot even agree among themselves. Fortunately the Christian and the Moslem do not quarrel over the same sites. To the Christian the most holy spot is the Church of the Holy Sepulchre. To the Moslem and to the Jew it is Mount Moriah. Whoever ultimately accepts responsibility for the government of Jerusalem must find the reconciliation of the sundry religious interests the most difficult problem presented for solution.

"Oh, pray for the peace of Jerusalem." How is the psalmist's craving henceforth to be fulfilled? Can any helpful lessons be deduced from our survey of the past? Situated as it is, Jerusalem can never hope to become the capital of a mighty empire. In its palmiest days it has been little more than the principal city of a paltry state. Its periods of independence under the successors of David, under the Maccabees, and under the Crusaders have been marked by constant wars, and struggles for existence. Comparative peace was only enjoyed while Palestine formed part of a powerful empire strong enough to keep off invaders. Thus it was in the days of the Romans, of the Arabs and of the Turks.

Palestine requires the strong arm of some one great power, which can preserve peace, and will hold the balance true between contending religions and creeds, and will allow all seekers after God to worship their Creator according to the light with which He has endowed them, and to visit those places which are eternally sacred.

"Oh, pray for the peace of Jerusalem; they shall prosper that love thee."

Appendix I

SOME USEFUL DATES

DATES prior to about 1000 B.C. could only be the roughest approximations and are therefore omitted.

B.C.
- 1000 David is reigning at Jerusalem.
- 938 Division of Judah and Israel.
- 929 Invasion of Judah by Shishak, Pharaoh of Egypt.
- 849 Revolt of Jehu.
- 733 Capture of Damascus by Tiglath-Pileser King of Assyria, and close of the Syrian kingdom.
- 722 Fall of Samaria, and destruction of the kingdom of Israel by the Assyrians under Shalmaneser.
- 711 Invasion of the Assyrians under Sennacherib.
- 608 Invasion of the Egyptians under Pharaoh Necho—Battle of Megiddo.
- 607 Capture of Jerusalem by the Babylonians under Nebuchadnezzar.
- 586 Destruction of Jerusalem and the Temple by the Babylonians and removal of the Jews into captivity at Babylon.
- 539 The Persians under Cyrus capture Babylon.
- 537 The Jews under Zerubbabel return to Jerusalem and rebuild the temple.
- 445 Nehemiah rebuilds the walls of Jerusalem.
- 333 Alexander defeats the Persians at the Battle of Issus.
- 323 Death of Alexander.
- 320 Capture of Jerusalem by Ptolemy I. king of Egypt.
- 301 Battle of Ipsus, after which Palestine is assigned to Ptolemy, and Syria to Seleucus I.

APPENDIX I

B.C.
- 198   Conquest of Palestine by Antiochus the Great.
- 170   Antiochus Epiphanes pollutes the temple at Jerusalem.
- 168   Revolt of the Jews under Mattathias.
- 166   Judas Maccabæus, son of Mattathias, founds the Maccabæan dynasty.
- 128   The Jews, under John Hyrcanus, recover their complete liberty.
- 63   Palestine conquered by the Romans under Pompey.
- 54   Temple of Jerusalem plundered by Crassus.
- 37   Herod the Great becomes king of the Jews.
- 4   Birth of Jesus Christ.
- 2   Death of Herod the Great.

A.D.
- 6   Palestine annexed to the Roman Empire.
- 24   Pontius Pilate appointed Governor of Palestine.
- 29   The Crucifixion of Jesus Christ.
- 70   Destruction of Jerusalem by Titus and dispersion of the Jews.
- 130   Jerusalem rebuilt by the Emperor Hadrian.
- 133   Revolt of the Jews under Simon Barcochebas.
- 335   The Empress Helena founds the Church of the Holy Sepulchre at Jerusalem. Under the Emperor Constantine Palestine comes into prominence as a Christian country.
- 614   Palestine is conquered by the Persians under Chosroes, who are subsequently driven out by the Christians under Heraclius.
- 637   Jerusalem is captured by the Arabs.
- 1075   Conquest of Palestine by the Turks.
- 1095–1099   The First Crusade, followed by the establishment of the Christian (Crusading) kingdom of Jerusalem.
- 1146–1149   The Second Crusade.
- 1187   Battle of Hattin—Overthrow of the Crusaders—Capture of Jerusalem by Saladin.
- 1189–1192   The Third Crusade.
- 1238   Capture of Jerusalem by the Turks.
- 1244   Capture of Jerusalem by the Kharezmians.
- 1291   Final expulsion of the Crusaders from Palestine.

APPENDIX I

A.D.
- 1400 Palestine conquered by Timoor the Tartar—(Tamberlane).
- 1517 Palestine annexed to the Ottoman Empire under Selim I.
- 1798 Napoleon invades Egypt.
- 1799 The French under Napoleon invade Palestine, but withdraw to Egypt.
- 1801 The British under Abercrombie expel the French from Egypt.
- 1805 Mehemet Ali proclaimed Pasha of Egypt.
- 1811 Massacre of the Mamelukes.
- 1831 Invasion of Syria by the Egyptians under Ibrahim, son and general of Mehemet Ali. The Ottoman Porte are restored to Syria, but Mehemet Ali and his heirs become hereditary rulers of Egypt.
- 1863 Ismail becomes Khedive of Egypt.
- 1869 Opening of the Suez Canal.
- 1879 Deposition of Ismail. Tewfik becomes Khedive of Egypt.
- 1882 Rebellion of the Egyptian army under Arabi Pasha leads to intervention, and the permanent military occupation of Egypt, by the British.
- 1914 Outbreak of the Great European War. British protectorate proclaimed over Egypt.
- 1915 The Turks invade Egypt and reach the Suez Canal.
- 1916 The British cross the Desert with the object of invading Palestine.
- 1917 Three battles are fought at Gaza, and Jerusalem surrenders to the British.
- 1918. Final overthrow of the Turkish army by the British, who complete the conquest of Palestine and Syria. Close of the Great European War.

Appendix II

LIST OF BOOKS

The Bible.
Ancient Egypt, by Canon Rawlinson. (T. Fisher Unwin.)
History of the Jews, by H. H. Milman. (Dent.)
Higher Criticism and the Verdict of the Monuments, by the Rev. A. H. Sayce, (S.P.C.K.)
From the Garden of Eden to the Crossing of the Jordan, by Sir Wm. Willcocks, K.C.M.G. (French Institute of Oriental Archæology.)
Historical Geography of the Holy Land, by George Adam Smith.
Sinai and Palestine, by Dean Stanley. (Murray.)
Josephus' Works, translated by Wm. Whiston, M.A. (Ward Lock & Co.)
Plutarch's Lives of Alexander and Pompey. (Ward Lock & Co.)
Jerusalem, by Col. Sir. C. M. Watson. (Dent.)
Alexander's Empire, by J. P. Mahaffy, D.D. (T. Fisher Unwin.)
The Caliphate: Its Rise, Decline and Fall, by Sir Wm. Muir, K.C.S.I. (Religious Tract Society.)
Jerusalem, the City of Herod and Saladin, by Walter Besant and E. H. Palmer. (Chatto & Windus.)
Egypt in the Nineteenth Century, by D. A. Cameron. (Smith, Elder & Co.)
Life of Napoleon I, by J. H. Rose. (Geo. Bell & Sons.)
Bonaparte's Campaign in Syria 1799, by G. S.I., E.E.F. (Government Press, Cairo.)
Macmillan's *Guides to Palestine and Egypt.* (Macmillan.)

INDEX

Abercrombie, 98
Aboukir, 98
Abu Bakr, 67
Abu Obeida, 70
Achan, 21
Acre, 83, 88, 90, 92, 96, 97
Adana, 77
Aelia Capitolina, 63
Agag, 30
Ahaz, 36
Ai, 21
Ajalon, 22
Akaba, 17
Aleppo, 11, 109, 111
Alexander the Great, 46
Alexandria, 101
Alexandrion, 53
Alexis, 75
Ali Muntar, 105
Amalekites, 30
Amenhotep, 11
Ammonites, 32
Antigonus, 48
Antiochus Epiphanes, 49
Antipater, 55
Antonia, 57, 62
Aphek, 29, 31
Arabi Pasha, 100
Arabs, 67
Arbela, 47
Archelaus, 56
Aristobolus, 52, 53
Arsuf, 88
Artaxerxes, 45
Ascalon, 86, 88
Assyria, 11, 34, 35, 37

Baalbek, 72
Babylon, 11, 35
Balaam, 19
Balak, 20
Baldwin, 77
Barak, 26

Barcochebas, 63
Beersheba, 18, 102, 107
Beirut, 89
Beisan, 71
Bernard, 82
Bethshan, 31
Bethshemesh, 30
Bitter Lakes, 15
Burgundy, Duke of, 89

Caesarea, 59
Cairo, 95
Cambyses, 44
Carchemish, 11
Cassius, 55
Cestius, 57
Children's Crusade, 91
Chosroes, 64
Constantine, 64
Constantinople, 64, 73
Crassus, 54
Crusades, 74
Cyprus, 44
Cyrus, 44

Damascus, 33, 70, 73, 84, 96, 110
Dardanelles, 103
Darum, 89
David, 31
Dead Sea, 19
Deborah, 26
Duma, 68

Edom, 19
Egypt, 7, 41
El Arish, 17, 96, 105
El Bireh, 21
El Khaweilifeh, 89
El Jib, 22
Elisha, 33
Emmaus, 31
Ephesus, 83
Esarhaddon, 40

INDEX

Esdraelon, 10, 26, 31, 33
Euphrates, 31, 41
Ezra, 45

Florus, 57
French, The, 93

Gaza, 9, 17, 28, 47, 96, 105, 106
Gibeon, 22
Gilgal, 21
Godfrey, 81
Gorgona, 76
Granicus, 46
Guy, 85

Hadrian, 63
Haifa, 27
Halicarnassus, 46
Hazor, 26
Hejaz, 73, 109
Heraclius, 64, 70
Hereopolis, 12
Herod, 55
Hezekiah, 38
Hims, 70
Hittites, 11
Hophni, 29
Hoshea, 37
Hyksos, 7
Hyrcanus, 52, 53

Ipsus, 48
Isaiah, 38
Ismail, 100
Issus, 47

Jabia, 72
Jabin, 26
Jael, 27
Jaffa, 89, 96, 107
Jaham, 9
Jamnia, 9
Jason, 49
Jehoiakim, 42
Jehu, 23
Jericho, 20, 109
Jeroboam, 32
Jerusalem, 19, 21, 31, 39, 40, 45, 58, 72, 79, 86, 107, 108
Jonathan, 52
Joppa, 48

Jordan, 20
Joseph, 7
Josephus, 59
Joshua, 20, 21
Josiah, 41
Julius Caesar, 55

Kadesh, 10, 12, 17, 18
Kantara, 104
Karnak, 32
Khalid, 68
Kishon, 26
Knight's Hospitallers, 82

Lachish, 38
Libya, 14
Ludd, 22, 88

Maccabees, 50
Mahomet, 66
Mameluke Sultans, 92, 93, 99
Manesseh, 40
Manna, 16
Marabout, 95
Mattathias, 50
Medes, 44
Media, 37
Medina, 109
Megiddo, 9, 10, 41
Mehemet Ali, 98
Menelaus, 49
Menephthah, 14
Mesopotamia, 11, 109
Michmash, 21
Midianites, 27
Mizpeh, 51, 108
Moab, 19
Moses, 16, 18
Mount Tabor, 97
Murat, 97

Naaman, 33
Naharain, 10
Napoleon, 94
Nebuchadnezzar, 42
Necho, 41
Nehemiah, 45
Nero, 57
Nile, 41
Nineveh, 47

INDEX

Nicea, Sultan of, 76
Nur ed Din, 84

Og, 19
Omar, 70
Oreb, 28
Orontes, 10, 12
Ottoman Empire, 93

Parthians, 55
Pekah, 36
Pelusium, 12, 39, 40, 45
Persia, 37
Persians, 44
Peter the Hermit, 74
Petra, 53
Philistia, 17, 38
Philippi, 55
Philistines, 29, 30
Phineas, 30
Phrygia, 77
Pompey, 53
Pontius Pilate, 56
Pope, 74
Port Said, 12, 39
Ptolemy, 48, 49

Rafa, 105
Rafat, 110
Rahab, 20
Rameses, II, 12
Ramleh, 22, 72, 78, 88
Raymond, 83, 85
Red Sea, 15
Rehoboam, 32
Rezin, 36
Richard I, 88, 89
Rhodes, 95
River of Egypt, 31
Rome, 53
Rutennu, 10, 11

Saladin, 83, 84, 90
Salmanna, 28
Samaria, 33, 37
Samson, 28
Samuel, 30
Sardis, 46

Saul, 30
Sefuriyeh, 85
Selim the Grim, 93
Seljuk Sultan, 84
Sennacherib, 37
Seti I, 12
Shalmaneser, 37
Shephelah, 30
Shepherd Kings, 7
Shishak, 32
Sihon, 19
Simon, 52
Sinai, 17
Sisera, 26
Solomon, 32
Sorek, 28
Soudan, 39
Suez Canal, 100, 102

Tadmor, 69
Tancred, 77
Tarsus, 77
Tartars, 92
Taurus, 11, 46, 77
Tehrak, 40
Tel el Kebir, 101
Templars, 81
Thothmes I., 7
  ,, II., 8
  ,, III., 9
Tiberias, 84
Tiglath Pileser, 36
Titus, 56, 58, 63
Tripoli, 78
Tyre, 47, 48, 85, 88

Uriah, 32

Vespasian, 58

Wacusa, 69
Wadi Surar, 28

Yarmuk, 67

Zeb, 28
Zeba, 28
Zedekiah, 42
Zerubabbel, 44, 45

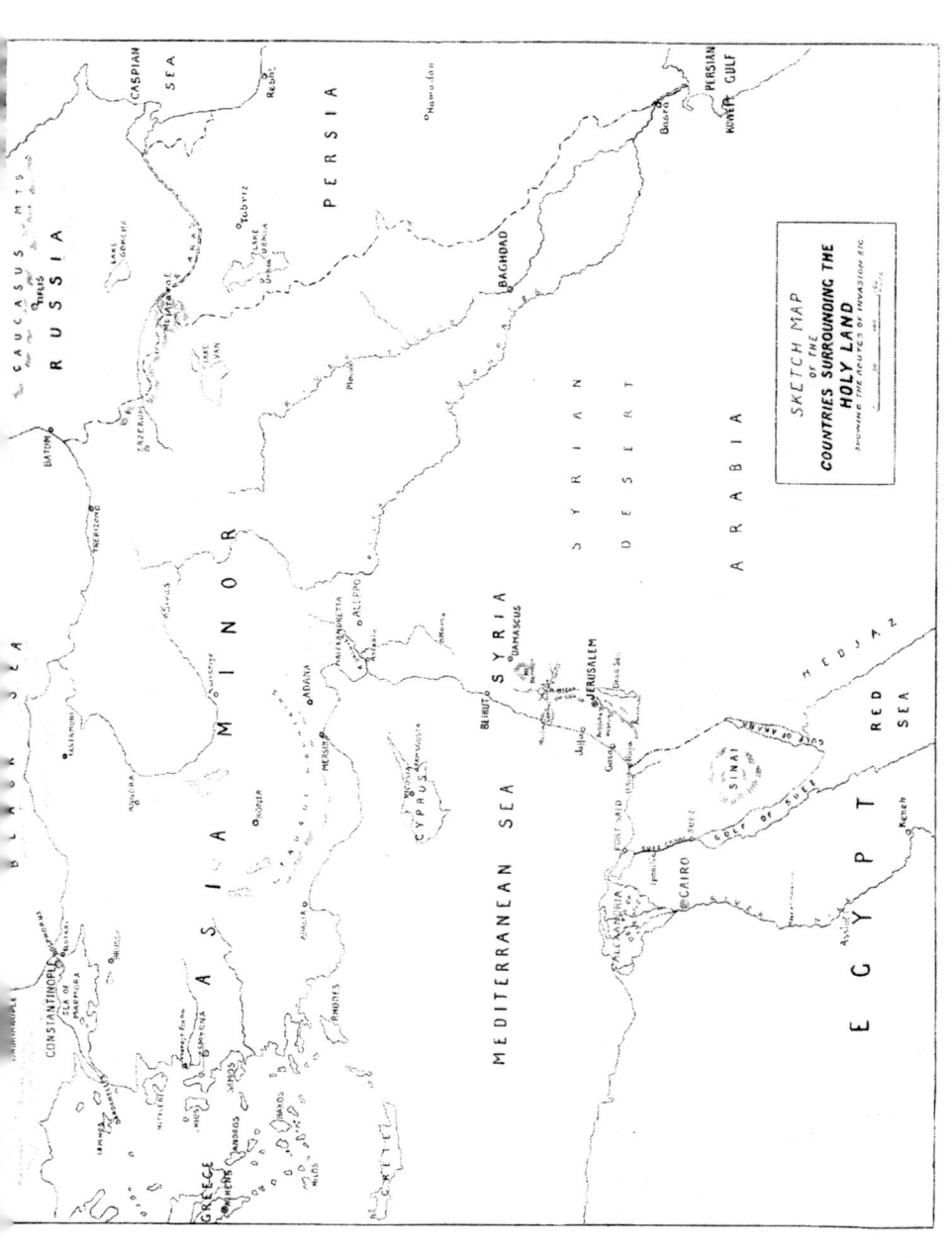

COSIMO is a specialty publisher of books and publications that inspire, inform, and engage readers. Our mission is to offer unique books to niche audiences around the world.

COSIMO BOOKS publishes books and publications for innovative authors, nonprofit organizations, and businesses. **COSIMO BOOKS** specializes in bringing books back into print, publishing new books quickly and effectively, and making these publications available to readers around the world.

COSIMO CLASSICS offers a collection of distinctive titles by the great authors and thinkers throughout the ages. At **COSIMO CLASSICS** timeless works find new life as affordable books, covering a variety of subjects including: Business, Economics, History, Personal Development, Philosophy, Religion & Spirituality, and much more!

COSIMO REPORTS publishes public reports that affect your world, from global trends to the economy, and from health to geopolitics.

FOR MORE INFORMATION CONTACT US AT
INFO@COSIMOBOOKS.COM

- ➢ if you are a book lover interested in our current catalog of books

- ➢ if you represent a bookstore, book club, or anyone else interested in special discounts for bulk purchases

- ➢ if you are an author who wants to get published

- ➢ if you represent an organization or business seeking to publish books and other publications for your members, donors, or customers.

COSIMO BOOKS ARE ALWAYS AVAILABLE AT ONLINE BOOKSTORES

**VISIT COSIMOBOOKS.COM
BE INSPIRED, BE INFORMED**

RVG
JAN
2025

CPSIA information can be obtained
at www.ICGtesting.com
Printed in the USA
FSOW01n2006231017
40266FS

9 781616 404963